MAUREEN CHADWICK

Maureen Chadwick is the creator and writer of a wide range of award-winning, critically acclaimed and controversial shows for both television and theatre, including single plays, primetime drama series, stage plays and musicals.

She was one of the co-founders and creative directors of Shed Productions, writing and producing a new wave of entertaining and hard-hitting television drama series, notably *Bad Girls*, *Footballers' Wives* and *Waterloo Road*.

Previous television credits include *Angels*, *EastEnders*, *Coronation Street* and BBC Screen One single dramas *Watch with Mother* and *Two Golden Balls*.

Previous theatre credits include *Joséphine* (at BAC and on national tour), *Dust* (BAC), *Bad Girls: The Musical* (at West Yorkshire Playhouse and in the West End), *The Speed Twins* (Riverside Studios) and *The Realness* (Hackney Downs Studios).

KATH GOTTS

Kath Gotts studied Philosophy and Psychology at St Hilda's College, Oxford, and then went on to study music at Goldsmiths College, London. She has written incidental music and songs for television and theatre, including *Bad Girls*, *The Fugitives*, *Family Affairs* and *Waterloo Road* on television and *Dust*, *The Bodies* and *Any Which Way* for theatre. She wrote the music and lyrics for *Bad Girls: The Musical*, with book by Maureen Chadwick and Ann McManus, which was produced at West Yorkshire Playhouse and at the Garrick Theatre in the West End. Her urban musical *The Realness*, with book by Maureen Chadwick and David Watson, premiered at Hackney Downs Studios in 2014, in a co-production with The Big House.

www.kathgotts.com

Book by
Maureen Chadwick

Music and Lyrics by
Kath Gotts

NICK HERN BOOKS
London
www.nickhernbooks.co.uk

A Nick Hern Book

Crush: The Musical first published in Great Britain in 2016 as a paperback original by Nick Hern Books Limited, The Glasshouse, 49a Goldhawk Road, London W12 8QP

Crush: The Musical copyright © 2016 Maureen Chadwick, Kath Gotts

Maureen Chadwick and Kath Gotts have asserted their moral right to be identified as the authors of this work

Cover photograph by David Ellis; Creative Design by Boom Ents (www.BoomEnts.com)

Designed and typeset by Nick Hern Books, London
Printed in Great Britain by CPI Books (UK) Ltd

A CIP catalogue record for this book is available from the British Library

ISBN   978 1 84842 558 3

Contents

The Making of *Crush: The Musical*
Kath Gotts

Crush: The Musical has had what is quite possibly a record-breakingly long gestation from conception to completion, one that's as much to do with the changing social attitudes of the last quarter of a century as it is the detours of our own professional lives.

The show was first conceived when I was not that long out of school uniform myself, when the tragicomic emotional territory of first love and adolescent angst was sadly rather fresh in my memory. Maureen and I decided we wanted to write a musical together and with our shared delight in Fred and Ginger movies we had a mission to write our own version of a romantic comedy in classic book-musical form. Inspired by our love of the British tradition of schoolgirl fiction – from Malory Towers to St Trinian's, and the old *Girl's Own* Annuals – we thought it would be great fun to write a musical set in that world. In fact, we were amazed that nobody else had got there before us and that here was this whole rich genre as yet unpilfered by musical-theatre writers, with its own distinctive milieu and lingo, and the schoolgirl crush providing new love story material for musical-comedy treatment.

With some early encouragement from Wendy Toye and Julian Slade we entered the very embryonic *Crush* (then called *Sugar and Spice*) for the 1989 Vivian Ellis Prize for New Musicals – three songs and a synopsis. We were thrilled to find we'd made it into the televised final. When asked to describe the show I cheerfully explained that it was a traditional romantic musical – just a simple case of 'girl meets girl, girl loses girl, one girl finds a boy and the other one finds another girl'. We'd heard that Cameron Mackintosh was rooting for us, but on the big day itself he unfortunately wasn't there in person and the rest of the panel seemed altogether perplexed by a love song from one schoolgirl to another – one suggested that he could imagine the show appealing to the 'old men in macs' brigade. As for Vivian

Ellis himself, he summed it up thus: 'At my old school of St Hilda's, it was, I always felt such talk was best confined to the locker room and that's all I have to say about that!'

Despite this first 'crushing blow' to our enthusiasm we continued to develop the show on our own. Justin Greene – then at the Nuffield Theatre, Southampton – read an early draft and gave us some positive feedback to keep going. But not only were we trying to write light-hearted musical comedy in an era of sung-through blockbuster musicals, we were specifically trying to write a mainstream musical comedy with a nascent lesbian love story in the homophobic era of Section 28. (The evil headmistress Miss Bleacher was our version of Margaret Thatcher, slashing budgets for arts education and espousing conservative 'family values' – despite the antics of her cabinet ministers.)

Of course, most of the cast of our 2015 production of *Crush* weren't even born in 1988 when Section 28 came into force, but this is why *Crush* isn't so much a musical *of* its time as a musical that has had to *wait* its time. Back in the late eighties and nineties the very notion of celebrating romantic love between schoolgirls was seen as radically subversive. (Remember, this was pre-Anna Friel's 'Beth Jordache' on *Brookside* back in 1994!)

Section 28 of the Local Government Act had stated that a local authority 'shall not intentionally promote homosexuality or publish material with the intention of promoting homosexuality' or 'promote the teaching in any maintained school of the acceptability of homosexuality as a pretended family relationship'. Although there were never any criminal prosecutions under this law it did create a climate of fear and uncertainty – particularly for those working with young people. The 1987 British Social Attitudes Survey revealed that seventy-five per cent of the population said that homosexual activity was 'always or mostly wrong', with only eleven per cent believing it to be never wrong.

It wasn't until 2003 that Section 28 was finally repealed – but how swiftly things have moved on since then, first with civil partnerships and then equal marriage. The relationship between public opinion and the law is, of course, a two-way street, with the law shaping public opinion as much as the other way around, and the world into which *Crush* has finally emerged all these years later would have been practically unimaginable when we started out. Indeed, our partnership with the charity Diversity Role Models to run anti-LGBT bullying workshops in schools shows just how far things have moved on.

Back in the dark days of the early nineties, however, we did pretty much consign *Crush* to Vivian Ellis's 'locker room' and left it there for a couple of decades as we got on with the rest of our lives. We did do a little workshop presentation at the East Dulwich Tavern in 1997, but by then Maureen was already writing for *Coronation Street*, which led on to *Bad Girls*, and then off and away on a twelve-year roller-coaster ride with Shed Productions. Meanwhile I was finishing my music degree and working for a charity, before swerving off into TV music writing and being Shed's first finance director! So, much though we would have hated to say so at the time, it was probably all for the best.

By 2004 we were workshopping *Bad Girls: The Musical*, another show for a predominantly female cast, which was first produced at West Yorkshire Playhouse in 2006, then transferred to the West End in 2007. And we're delighted that it's since become a hit with am-dram societies and drama colleges, both in the UK and around the world, and had its first professional revival at the Union Theatre in Southwark in March 2016.

But over the years we'd kept on singing 'Navy Knicks' and some of those early songs and thinking fondly of our abandoned musical in the bottom drawer. Finally, after she had left Shed Productions, Maureen decided it was time to take another look at it. Although fully expecting to have the usual cringe-making experience that goes with re-reading your juvenilia, she was delighted to discover how fresh it still seemed – as if all that youthful excitement and energy we'd first put into it was preserved intact, and the characters were just waiting to burst back into life. We knew we still loved its rebel spirit and felt it really captured something – an essence of schoolgirl passion, idealism and silliness. So we decided to start work in earnest to develop the original material into the musical we always wanted it to be. And, of course, we were much better equipped to take on that task than we would have been twenty years previously.

A ruthless process of rewriting ensued – songs cut, new ones added, existing songs reworked and the whole script and structure thoroughly nipped, tucked and polished. A workshop presentation of the new improved *Crush* at the Harold Pinter Theatre in October 2013 allowed us to get a good sense of seeing the show on its feet and in front of an audience – and from that we gathered a great deal of useful feedback for yet another round of revisions and additions…

Of course, when working on pre-existing material there's always a risk that changing one small element will send the whole pack of cards tumbling down, so it's been a delicate balance. But the final sessions of detailed scriptwork with the director prior to rehearsals allowed us to unearth the last few remaining 'bodies under the patio' and make sure everything locked together in the most lively fashion ready for its premiere in 2015.

It's wonderful to have arrived at a time when the show can be widely enjoyed for what it is – a light but big-hearted and universal story about growing up, facing adversity and learning to be true to yourself. And we really hope that everyone who performs *Crush* or goes to see it will get as much fun out of it as we've tried to put into it.

Acknowledgements

In addition to all those who worked on the Belgrade Theatre production of *Crush*, the authors would like to thank the numerous colleagues and friends who have helped to take *Crush* on its long journey over the years – with particular acknowledgement to: Nikki Slade, James McConnell, Maggie Norris, Neil McArthur, Janet Prince, Sarah Travis, Gareth Valentine, Thom Southerland and Justin Greene – to name but a few.

Crush and the Girls' School Story
Professor Rosemary Auchmuty FRSA

The popularity of girls' school stories has always been an embarrassing enigma to mainstream critics. It is often claimed that Thomas Hughes's *Tom Brown's School Days* (1857) was the first British school story, with girls' school stories following only after educational opportunities were extended to girls in the later nineteenth century. In fact, Sarah Fielding's *The Governess, or The Little Female Academy* (1749) preceded *Tom Brown* by more than a century, and girls' school stories have always been more significant than boys' in terms of number of titles, popularity and sales.

There is a good reason for this. Prior to the mid-nineteenth century, middle-class girls were denied an academic education and were trained instead in the feminine virtues to be helpmates of men. The girls' school story as we know and love it was a product of the early feminist movement to create educational opportunities for women in schools and universities and to fit them for paid employment and independent lives. Far from being the embodiment of respectability, restrictiveness and outmoded values that they later came to represent, the schools – the girls' high schools and the public schools like Cheltenham Ladies' College, Wycombe Abbey and Roedean – were radical and feminist in their recognition that knowledge is power and their insistence that girls be educated beyond married dependence. The books captured this spirit and so does *Crush*, where the founder's suffragette vision is contrasted to the interloper headmistress's invocation of regressive 'Victorian values'.

The authors of girls' school stories were themselves beneficiaries of this emancipation through education: jobbing writers in the main, they supplied an eager, growing market of school and working girls with a product at first viewed as harmless, if not morally sound and character-building. Their readers were generally girls who did not (and would not have been able to) attend the deliciously attractive boarding schools depicted, who received the books as school or Sunday-school prizes and later, drawn into the fantasy world, saved their pocket money to buy additions to their favourite series or requested them as birthday or Christmas presents. No one took much notice of their innocent pleasure until the subversive power of girls' school stories began to be recognised just before the Second World War and the backlash began. Within a decade the genre had been practically wiped off the publishers' lists, and those girls who had loved the books, and the women who went on loving them, had to fall back on nostalgia and the second-hand market.

Why have so many girls and women (and some men) loved the books, even up to the present day? And why did the books have to be denigrated and forcibly suppressed? The answer to both questions is the same. We loved them, and they had to go, because they depicted all-women worlds in which men were not the centre of women's existence – were, indeed, largely decorative or superfluous – and where women could occupy any and every role requiring skill, courage and leadership. Naturally, in a patriarchy, this is quite wrong: women should be followers, not leaders; women should be dependent and in need of protection, not independent and brave; women should devote themselves to men, not to self-development or – God forbid – to other girls or women.

The destruction of girls' school stories took many forms. One was the reinterpretation of the 'crush', the focus of this musical. In early school stories, such as those by Angela Brazil, girls' hero-worship of other girls or mistresses is treated simply as a plot device typical of girls' schools, quite neutrally, but in the 1920s, under the influence of the new 'science' of sexology, it came to be decried as *immature* and, later, *unhealthy*. It took the sophisticated parodies of male satirists like Lord Berners (*The Girls of Radcliff Hall*, 1936), Philip Larkin and Arthur Marshall to make an overt link with sexual deviance, but the critics quickly took this up, and by the 1970s everyone was sniggering at the 'lesbian' content of so many of these books. 'One must assume that these authors... had not the faintest idea in this instance what they were writing about,' observed Gillian Avery in *Childhood's Pattern* (1975). In fact, I suggest, these authors knew very well that they were writing about love between women, but did not see it as pathological.

Many school-story enthusiasts have mixed feelings about the masculine camping-up of school life in Arthur Marshall and Co.'s work, which often seems to mock rather than celebrate women and their all-female world. When women write such parodies, however, the tone is more sympathetic: Nancy Spain's *Poison for Teacher* (1949) (also set in 'Radcliff Hall', in this case based on her own school, Roedean) casts a critical but indulgent eye on both the institution and the genre; she was certainly writing consciously as an insider and a lesbian. Different again, because possible now, is the approach in *Crush*, where the lesbian content is neither satirised nor parodied: rather, it is central to the narrative and resolution of the school's fight to defend its progressive values.

Fans of girls' school stories will recognise many of the motifs in this show: the tyrannical replacement headmistress, the benefactors in disguise, the girls who run away and the school sneak who redeems herself. But the humour is also characteristic of the later school stories. As Sue Sims has noted in *The Encyclopaedia of Girls' School Stories* (2000), it is a mark of maturity when authors feel free to mock established institutions that matter to them. Sims locates the shift in treatment in the later interwar and post-war period, which many consider to be their golden age, when girls' school stories become 'deliberately funny; the idealism and seriousness of many of the 1920s books are gently held up to ridicule'. At the same time, the ironic tone masks the original steely message: that education matters, that girls matter, that women matter, for themselves and not simply in relation to men. The books kept their popularity through the second half of the twentieth century because this message became ever more important, and it is a message that still resonates forcefully today.

Professor Rosemary Auchmuty is the author of *A World of Girls: The Appeal of the Girls' School Story* (London: The Women's Press, 1992, 2nd ed.2004) and *A World of Women: Growing Up in the Girls' School Story* (London: The Women's Press, 1999, 2nd ed. 2008).

Crush: The Musical was first performed at the Belgrade Theatre Coventry on 4 September 2015 and toured to Brighton Theatre Royal and Richmond Theatre. The cast was as follows:

MISS AUSTIN	Sara Crowe
JUDITH	Eleanor Brown
DAIMLER JONES	Brianna Ogunbawo
ANNABEL	Catherine Hayworth
CAMILLA FARADAY	Charlotte Miranda-Smith
SUSAN SMART	Stephanie Clift
LAVINIA	Emma Harrold
BRENDA SMEARS	Georgia Oldman
SWING	Jennifer Potts
DORIAN/'BENNY'	James Meunier
MISS BLEACHER	Rosemary Ashe
DIANA DOSSERDALE/ 'MISS GIVINGS'	Kirsty Malpass

Director	Anna Linstrum
Designer	David Farley
Lighting Designer	Johanna Town
Choreographer	Richard Roe
Orchestration & Musical Supervision	Steven Edis
Musical Director	Helen Ireland
Sound Designer	Ben Harrison

Produced by Douglas McJannet on behalf of Big Broad Productions in association with the Belgrade Theatre, Coventry.

Book by
Maureen Chadwick

Music and Lyrics by
Kath Gotts

Characters
in order of appearance

MISS AUSTIN, *the deputy headmistress*

THE UPPER SIXTH
JUDITH, *the head girl*
DAIMLER JONES, *the trusty and true*
ANNABEL, *the American beatnik*
CAMILLA FARADAY, *the heartbreaker*
SUSAN SMART, *the romantic*
LAVINIA, *the debutante*
BRENDA SMEARS, *the school sneak*

'BENNY', *the odd-job boy*
MISS BLEACHER, *the headmistress*
'MISS GIVINGS', *the temporary games mistress*
DIANA DOSSERDALE, *niece of Dame Dorothea*
DORIAN DOSSERDALE, *nephew of Dame Dorothea*
MR *and* MRS SMART, *Susan's parents*
'BUZZ BRAKELAST', *guardian angel*
'MARLENE DIETRICH'
'CAMILLE', *a French waitress*
'DESIREE JONES', *a nightclub chanteuse*
'DAME DOROTHEA DOSSERDALE', *the school's founder*

And PASSERS-BY AND CLUB-GOERS

Casting Note

Minimum cast size of eleven (ten female, one male), with no covers.

Characters in inverted commas are either in disguise or as imagined in Susan's dream sequence – e.g. Buzz Brakelast must be recognisable as Miss Givings/Diana Dosserdale.

Susan's parents can either be doubled by the same actors who play Dorian and Diana Dosserdale, or they may be cast as separate roles if a larger cast size is required.

There are seven character roles in the Upper Sixth, but additional schoolgirls may be added to the ensemble as desired.

Authors' Note

Crush is inspired by the classic schoolgirl-story tradition and its delightful combination of silliness and spirit, noble ideals and passionate friendships – and to be both funny and emotionally engaging it needs to be performed with utmost sincerity. Any temptation to send up the characters should be steadfastly resisted.

4

Musical Numbers

Music 16	**What If?** – Desiree and Trio
Music 16a	**Fly in the Germolene** – instrumental
Music 16b	**What Would Dottie Do?** – instrumental
Music 17	**You Do Do the Magic for Me** – Susan and Daimler
Music 17a	**Switch the Snitch** – instrumental
Music 18	**Do Your Bit** – Miss Austin, Dame Dorothea and Upper Sixth
Music 18a	**Do Your Bit** – play-off instrumental
Music 19	**I Ask for Nothing** – Miss Bleacher
Music 20	**The School Song/Best Days** reprise – full company (excl. Miss Bleacher)
Music 21	**Bows/Navy Knicks/Curtain** – instrumental/full company
Music 22	**Playout** – instrumental

Note on Music

Song lyrics are in bold text.

The full score, with lyrics and music by Kath Gotts and arranged by Steven Edis, is available from Nick Hern Books (see details on page iv).

The arrangement is for a seven-piece band including Keyboard/Musical Director.

The other chairs are:
Keyboard 2
Woodwind (trebling: clarinet, alto sax, baritone sax)
Guitar (trebling: acoustic, electric, ukulele)
Violin (also doubling mandolin)
Bass (doubling: bass guitar and double bass)
Percussion, comprising:
    kit (BD, SD, 3 toms, HH, crash cym, ride cym, splash/choke cym)
    tambourine, temple blocks, woodblock, cowbell
    castanets, timbales, small chinese tomtom
    shaker, guiro, sleighbells, mark tree, triangle
    washboard, glockenspiel

6

ACT ONE

Music. **Overture**

Prologue

Music 1. **The Best Days of Our Lives**

Dead of night. A lamp illuminates a desk, where an elderly lady,
MISS AUSTIN, *sits, writing an urgent letter.*

UPPER SIXTH (*off*).
　　School, we don't want to go
　　School, we don't want to know
　　School
　　Hmmm... (*Continuing under.*)

MISS AUSTIN. To the Dosserdale Trust, care of Messrs.
　　Puttifoot and Partners, Solicitors. September Twenty-Fifth,
　　Nineteen Sixty-Three...

　　Dear sirs... As you will be aware, our recently deceased and
　　dearly missed principal, Dame Dorothea Dosserdale,
　　established this school in the belief that equal access to
　　education was the true gateway to emancipation. But I beg to
　　inform you that the key is no longer in safe hands...

　　She stops –

UPPER SIXTH (*off*).
　　Dark and depressed days
　　All we detest days
　　Whatever happened to the best days of our lives?
　　Whatever happened to them?
　　School
　　Hmmm... (*Continuing under.*)

　　MISS AUSTIN *starts again.*

MISS AUSTIN. Dear sirs... I trust you will not need to be
　　reminded that this school's founding mission was to inspire

young women from all walks of life to cultivate their unique talents and go forth to fulfil their dreams. But we are now under the heel of what can only be described as a jackboot...

She stops –

UPPER SIXTH (*off*).
> **Feeling oppressed days**
> **Beating our breast days**
> **Whatever happened to the best days of our lives?**
> **Whatever happened – ?**

MISS AUSTIN *throws caution to the wind.*

MISS AUSTIN. Dear sirs, this is an SOS message. Please Save Our School from imminent catastrophe.

Transition:

Song continues as a new day dawns at...

Dame Dorothea Dosserdale School for Girls, England, 1963.

Scene One

The school quad – Wednesday morning, one week later.

The Upper Sixth boarders – DAIMLER, JUDITH, ANNABEL, LAVINIA, SUSAN and CAMILLA – assemble for roll-call in doom-impassioned protest.

UPPER SIXTH.
> **We used to be raring to go**
> **Every morning half-past eight**
> **But now we don't want to know**
> **We're yawning and we're late**
> **Doom and gloom in every room**
> **We've lost our youthful bloom**
> **How could anyone condemn us to this fate?**
>
> **We used to jump up in the air**
> **When we heard that school bell ring**

Freewheeling devil-may-care
Every girl could do her thing
Dancing barefoot on the grass
Boaters on then off to class
What a cavalcade of joy each day would bring

Now those were the best days
Heavenly blessed days
Whatever happened to the best days of our lives?
Whatever happened to them?
Sparkle-and-zest days
Riding-the-crest days
Whatever happened to the best days of our lives?

Funereal gloom resumes.

Farewell that gay Arcadia
Of happy girlhood
All those who laughed and played here
Like every girl should
Those days are gone, alas, alack
Those days are gone and won't be back
Goodbye
The best days of our lives
Goodbye
The best days of our lives.

All are slumped in despair, as MISS AUSTIN, *the deputy head, enters on her bicycle.*

MISS AUSTIN. Girls, girls, girls… This is hardly a good example to set the First Years, is it?

JUDITH. Sorry, Miss Austin –

DAIMLER. Dear Miss Austin –

ANNABEL. But you dig what's dragging us cats down –

CAMILLA. The beyond-beastly Miss Bleacher –

SUSAN. Headmistress from Hell –

LAVINIA. And she's only been here three weeks!

MISS AUSTIN. Oh tut tut, saddle up…

> You should know better than this my dears
> What have I told you all these years?
> No matter what may portend
> We have to face it
> And see it through to the end
> The Dosserdalian Way

UPPER SIXTH.
> The Dosserdalian Way

MISS AUSTIN.
> Open your arms to the day

MISS AUSTIN/UPPER SIXTH.
> And embrace it

MISS AUSTIN.
> These days they may not be the best
> But every day must be addressed
> Believing in the best of the rest of your lives

MISS AUSTIN/UPPER SIXTH.
> Bring back the best days
> Sparkle-and-zest days
> Riding-the-crest days
> We will see those days again
> Freely expressed days
> Just be-my-guest days
> Oblige-noblessed days
> On-with-our-quest days
> Roll on the best days of our lives.

School bell rings.

MISS AUSTIN *ushers the* UPPER SIXTH *into school, all with heavy hearts but heads held high.*

CAMILLA *takes* SUSAN *by the arm and whisks her aside.*

CAMILLA. Darling, don't let's suffer assembly. It's too, too tedious.

SUSAN. But darling, you heard Miss Austin. We have to be stoic.

CAMILLA. No we don't. We can leave that to the drones and be divinely à deux in the locker room.

SUSAN. And risk getting another detention off Bleacher?

CAMILLA. My mother says if self-expression is now a sin, detentions are the new merits. The more I get the prouder she'll be.

SUSAN. You're lucky. All my parents want me to get is straight As and a scholarship to Oxford.

CAMILLA. Yawn.

SUSAN. No one else in my whole family's ever had the chance to go to university before.

CAMILLA. Sigh.

SUSAN. Couldn't we just wait until break?

CAMILLA. Wait?

She recoils, clutching her heart.

Oh, l'amour, l'amour! Je suis désolée!

CAMILLA *flounces off.* SUSAN *flusters, torn – then scurries after her.*

BRENDA SMEARS, *the school sneak, pops up from her hiding place – squinting after them and jotting in her notebook.*

BRENDA. 'Oh l'amour – l'amour – je suis désolée…'

Then she's hailed by a whistle and BENNY *enters – a cheeky young chappie dressed as a workman with tool bag.*

BENNY. Wotcher, darlin'! Awright? Betcha chuffed to clock me wiv me big wrench at the ready, aintcha!

BRENDA. Pardon me?

BENNY. Well jus' point us the way to yer showers, I'll have a butcher's and Bob's your uncle – (*Clicks his tongue and winks.*) know what I mean?

BRENDA. I don't have the faintest clue. Who are you?

BENNY. I'm Benny the Bag, ain't I?

BRENDA. I don't know. Are you?

BENNY. In the flesh. I'm from the Odd Job Agency. Got a list as long as me arm what needs seeing to 'ere… (*Unfurls a roll of paper from his bag.*) Number one being your hot water's gone on the blink, yeah?

BRENDA. No it hasn't, it's been turned off. And I'm very busy. Goodbye.

She makes to leave. He pursues.

BENNY. Eh, you what? Just a sec. You ain't telling me it's been turned off like deliberately on purpose?

BRENDA. By Miss Bleacher, our new headmistress. Because cold showers are character-building.

BENNY (*Cockney accent slips*). Crikey! (*Corrects himself.*) I mean, cor blimey stone the crows!

I don't Adam an' Eve it! Dame Dotty Dossers? Sposed to be one o' them whacky, anyfink goes, ahead o' the times type o' schools, aintcha?

BRENDA. That's why Miss Bleacher's changed our school motto from 'Age quod agis' to 'Disce aut discede'.

BENNY. Eh?

BRENDA. Don't you speak Latin? It means instead of softy-wafty 'Do what you do well', it's now strictly 'Learn or depart'. Because schools without rules breed savages and socialists.

She dashes off. BENNY *shakes his head after her.*

BENNY. Nuff said, yeah…

Music 1a. **Gay Arcadia**

He removes a camera from his tool bag and takes snaps, then makes his own furtive way into the school.

Scene Two

Assembly hall.

A portrait of Dame Dorothea Dosserdale in Suffragette costume looks upwards and onwards.

A wall plaque displays the school badge with new motto 'Disce Aut Discede'.

The UPPER SIXTH – *featuring* JUDITH, LAVINIA, DAIMLER, ANNABEL – *and* MISS AUSTIN *stand to attention as* MISS BLEACHER *makes her entrance… and* BENNY *gets busy up a ladder nearby, stealthily removing a microphone from his bag.*

MISS BLEACHER (*to auditorium*). Good morning, girls.

SCHOOL. Good-morn-ing, Miss-Bleach-er.

MISS BLEACHER. Our theme in assembly this week is Duty.

And today we shall consider the duties incumbent upon you as members of this school and the society you are preparing to serve.

Music 2. **The Future Mothers of the Future Sons of England**

So let us begin by asking ourselves –

What is the function of an upright member?

A stifled snigger from LAVINIA.

**An upright member of this school
Sadly in the past
Questions such as these
Were very rarely asked
So ladies – your attention please…**

Character is destiny. And hard work and discipline will shape yours…

**The future mothers of the future sons of England
Indeed the breeders of our leaders yet to come
For who knows if one fine day**

A Prime Minister might say
To one who's here amongst us: 'Dearest Mum'

The future mothers of the future sons of England
You're here to learn so they in turn fulfil their dreams
They'll be healthy, hale and hearty
Never frail and never arty
The captains of our county cricket teams

The military or industry, parliament or law
The extent of their ascent is planted firmly at your door
There could be no finer, higher call
It is a woman's moral duty above all

MISS AUSTIN/UPPER SIXTH.
Oh, oh, oh, oh, oh, oh, oh, oh... (*Continuing under.*)

MISS BLEACHER.
The future mothers of the future sons of England
You live your lives to be the wives of greater men
Your role to stand beside them
Cajole and gently guide them
Then reproduce their greatness once again –

MISS AUSTIN/UPPER SIXTH.
Oh no, oh no, oh no –

MISS BLEACHER.
And again –
And again...
Though I myself did not give birth
I know my mission here on earth
Proudly to promulgate this rule...

MISS AUSTIN/UPPER SIXTH.
Oh no, oh no, oh no –

MISS BLEACHER.
We strive to educate
So you may better procreate
And that henceforth shall be –
The function of this school

Disce aut discede.

The function of this school.

The UPPER SIXTH *and* MISS AUSTIN *are left reeling in shock.*

As members of the Upper Sixth may surmise, you will have much to learn *before* you depart – hence all your extra-curricular activities will be replaced forthwith by compulsory Homecraft.

A collective intake of breath – and a lone voice blurts out.

DAIMLER. Homecraft?!

MISS BLEACHER *twitches*.

MISS BLEACHER. Do I detect a dissenting voice?

MISS AUSTIN *tries to deflect*.

MISS AUSTIN. Old habits, Headmistress –

MISS BLEACHER *narrows her sights on the culprit*.

MISS BLEACHER. Name?

DAIMLER *steps forth*.

DAIMLER. Um – Daimler Jones, Miss.

MISS BLEACHER. Ah yes, Daimler… you're one of our very lucky charity girls from the orphanage. Presumably named after the stolen car in which your own unfit mother conceived you.

MISS AUSTIN. Daimler is a scholar sans pareil, Headmistress, and thrice-times captain of our winning team in the Annual Inter-Schools Debating Society Contest.

MISS BLEACHER. Oh dear.

DAIMLER. But I wouldn't have a voice at all if this school hadn't helped me find it, Miss Bleacher. And that's why I want to use my education to nurture the future *daughters* of England.

MISS AUSTIN. Daimler means to rejoin our ranks as a member of staff, Headmistress, upon completion of her doctorate.

MISS BLEACHER. Really? Then you won't want to blot your copybook before you even matriculate. Will you?

MISS AUSTIN *leans in*.

MISS AUSTIN. I'll have a private word.

MISS BLEACHER. Good. (*To auditorium*.) And let every girl
here take heed, given the depravity now raging amongst us...
(*Collects herself*.) Suffice to say I have been obliged to
investigate a complaint from the domestic staff concerning
Indecent and Unnatural Behaviour in the art room after hours
by two members of the upper school.

The UPPER SIXTH *and* MISS AUSTIN *are jolted anew*.

Their identities are as yet unknown, but let their friends and
fellows be in no doubt: to conceal a sin is to share the guilt.
And you too will be found out.

Tyrannical pause.

We shall now sing hymn number four hundred and eighty-
one in your hymn books.

Piano starts up.

MISS AUSTIN. Um, Headmistress –

MISS BLEACHER. What?

MISS AUSTIN *whispers something*.

Oh, that – (*To pianist*.) Just one minute, Miss MacLaren,
please –

Piano pauses.

(*To auditorium*.) One further notice –

Piano carries on.

(*To pianist*.) Miss MacLaren? (*Shouts*.) Miss MacLaren!

Piano jolts to a halt.

Put your hearing aid in. (*To auditorium*.) One further notice,
regarding staff shortfall in the PE Department. The school is
fortunate in having obtained the temporary services of Miss
– (*Looks to* MISS AUSTIN.)

MISS AUSTIN. Givings.

MISS BLEACHER. Miss Givings, who will be taking all games periods for the remainder of the term.

(*To pianist*.) Take it away, Miss MacLaren.

Piano resumes.

Music 3. **Hymn No. 481**

MISS AUSTIN/MISS BLEACHER/UPPER SIXTH.
    Weak and unworthy sinners all are we
    Humbly we surrender never more to be
    Wayward in our hearts, Lord, straying from thy path
    Lead us unto righteousness and spare us thy wrath

    Fear and forbearance shall our watchwords be
    Resting not in idleness, striving steadfastly
    Pure must be our thoughts, Lord, vengeful be thy sword
    Vanquish thou our sinfulness upon thy word
    Blah, blah, blah, blah, blah... (*Etc*.)

They exit singing, MISS AUSTIN *beckoning* DAIMLER *under her wing, and all except for* MISS BLEACHER *switch to 'blah, blah' lyrics as soon as possible.*

Meanwhile, BENNY *switches off a portable tape recorder inside his bag and sneaks off separately.*

Scene Three

Locker room.

A row of bath towels hangs from hooks above a bench, with a large cupboard and lockers nearby.

SUSAN *enters, searching for* CAMILLA, *who is hiding behind one of the towels.*

BRENDA *sneaks in soon after, to hide behind another towel.*

During the song, BRENDA *shifts from one hiding place to another in her efforts to spy on them – only narrowly escaping discovery herself – and she is continually thwarted, as* CAMILLA *stays obscured from her view and she only ever catches direct sight of* SUSAN.

SUSAN. Oh, darling, where are you? Oh, what do you want me to say? Shall I compare thee to a summer's day? Being your slave, what should I do but tend upon the hours and times of your desire?

CAMILLA *flings the towel aside and flounces.*

CAMILLA. Of course you *should*. But instead you chose to tend upon the hours of the school timetable.

SUSAN. Oh, darling, please forgive me. You know I love you with all my heart.

CAMILLA. Well, that's not enough, is it?

Music 4. **Totally, Utterly, Truly**

**Do you totally utterly truly and madly adore me?
Were you all in a spin of excitement the minute you
  saw me?
Do you love me a million, a billion, a trillion, a zillion –**

SUSAN.

**Times infinity
Heart on my sleeve
Darling please believe
You're the only girl for me
But if I sing your praise for the rest of my days, won't
  it bore you?**

CAMILLA.
>I could never get tired of being admired I assure you

SUSAN.
>Then I'll love you forever and ever and ever and ever
>>and ever and a day
>Faithful and true
>My whole life through

CAMILLA/SUSAN.
>Forever we'll be toujours gai

SUSAN.
>I'm just a hopeless romantic
>Who's frantic
>To tell everyone how wonderful you are
>There's no other girl here
>To come near
>You're miles above the rest of them by far

CAMILLA.
>It's such fun feeling like this

SUSAN.
>>Without you I know I would surely die

CAMILLA.
>On the run and stealing a kiss

SUSAN.
>>With you I'm so happy I could cry

CAMILLA.
>Hiding our illicit affair

SUSAN.
>>You're absolutely
>>Marvellously, perfect for me

CAMILLA.
>And if they find out
>I simply won't care
>Because I know that you totally utterly truly adore me

SUSAN.
>If you weren't there life would be unbearable for me
>I love you a million

CAMILLA.
Billion

SUSAN.
Trillion

CAMILLA.
Zillion

CAMILLA/SUSAN.
Times infinity

SUSAN.
You're my life, my death
You're my every breath
And I'll never –

CAMILLA.
Never –

SUSAN.
Never –

CAMILLA.
Never –

SUSAN.
Never –

CAMILLA.
Never –

CAMILLA/SUSAN.
Ever be free
And that's totally utterly truly madly wonderful
For me –

SUSAN.
For me –

CAMILLA.
For me –

SUSAN.
For me –

CAMILLA/SUSAN.
For me.

They fall into a stagey embrace and kiss – as a loud sneeze erupts from inside the cupboard.

What was that?

CAMILLA *hides, leaving* SUSAN *on the spot, as* BRENDA *falls out of the cupboard in a jumble of hockey sticks.*

SUSAN. Brenda?!

BRENDA *bolts.*

CAMILLA. Who?

SUSAN. Bleacher's pet, Brenda Smears.

CAMILLA. Since when would that servile little swot dare to bunk off assembly?

SUSAN. She must have been snooping on us all this while.

CAMILLA. Don't credit her with a purpose, darling. She was probably solving some dreary theorem and lost all track of space and time.

SUSAN. In the games-equipment cupboard?

CAMILLA. Well, maybe she was searching for the secret door back to the goblin world. I'd much prefer to contemplate a thing of beauty.

She flips open a compact case to reapply lipstick, as SUSAN *tidies up the hockey sticks, and* JUDITH, LAVINIA *and* ANNABEL *enter in a babble of despair.*

JUDITH. So now we know the worst.

LAVINIA. It's even worse than we thought.

ANNABEL. It's like Hellsville, man.

JUDITH. I bet even the damned are allowed to have a Debating Society and an end-of-term discotheque.

LAVINIA. We don't have minds of our own at all.

JUDITH. We're just breeding stock.

LAVINIA. With a duty to spy on each other!

ANNABEL. Yeah, scratch H-ville. We're on the wrong side of the tracks in Zombie Town.

SUSAN *and* CAMILLA *are bemused.*

SUSAN. Why, what's up now?

LAVINIA. Your number, mes amies, if you don't watch out.

SUSAN. What do you mean?

JUDITH. The purge is on.

LAVINIA. Every girl must answer the call.

ANNABEL. Death to deviants, one and all.

They mime slitting throats.

CAMILLA (*to* SUSAN). What are they talking about?

DAIMLER *enters with her head in a poetry book.*

SUSAN. Daimler, tell us! What's happened?

DAIMLER. Oh, nothing much. Bleacher's gone off on a full-blown moral crusade. And thanks to your antics in the art room, you're her number-one target.

SUSAN *turns to* CAMILLA *in alarm.*

SUSAN. That batty old cleaner bursting in on us…

CAMILLA. It's not our fault she went into shock. She should have knocked.

SUSAN. And we tried to explain that naked body painting was an avant-garde conceptual art form.

DAIMLER. You're just lucky she didn't know who you were. But Bleacher's told the whole school we've got to turn you in.

JUDITH. Which obviously we won't.

LAVINIA. As if?

ANNABEL. Like drop dead, daddy-o!

DAIMLER. But we all know who would, so –

SUSAN. Oh no – (*To* CAMILLA.) That means Brenda Smears *was* spying on us.

DAIMLER. Where? When?

SUSAN. Here. Just now.

DAIMLER. Oh, Susan! Didn't I warn you not to take stupid risks?

SUSAN. But we didn't have a clue until she fell out of the cupboard!

CAMILLA. Et obvs ergo ditto *she* won't have a clue about *us*.

DAIMLER. You hope.

CAMILLA *snubs* DAIMLER *and steers* SUSAN *aside*.

CAMILLA. This is simply too sordid for words, darling.

All GIRLS *proceed to change into games kit during the following*.

JUDITH. Our dear Dame Dottie must be tossing in her grave.

LAVINIA. She must have gone potty to leave us with Bleacher.

DAIMLER*'s patience snaps*.

DAIMLER. Oh please at least get your facts right.

LAVINIA. Excusez-moi?

DAIMLER. You can't blame the Dame for that. It was her senile brother – Sir Digby Dosserdale – he left us with Bleacher.

JUDITH/LAVINIA. Comment cela?

DAIMLER. Haven't you ever read the school constitution?

ANNABEL/JUDITH//LAVINIA. Quoi?

DAIMLER (*sighs*). Dame Dottie and Sir Digby were our joint founders – Dottie had the vision but Digby had the money. So when Dame Dottie passed away this summer, all the power passed on to demented Sir Digby – and he passed over Miss Austin and picked Bleacher as our new Head.

JUDITH. Then I wish he was tossing in *his* grave.

DAIMLER. Well, tossing or not, he's in it. It said in the paper he died last week. Which means our fate now lies with the two next-of-kin.

ANNABEL. Yeah? So who are *these* guys?

DAIMLER. His niece and nephew – the love children of Dame Dottie's twin sister Daphne, who perished in the Punjab. And Miss Austin's already written to their solicitors about our plight.

The trio perk up.

ANNABEL/JUDITH//LAVINIA. Hope revives!

DAIMLER. But she fears they may be too busy living exciting lives of their own.

The trio slump.

ANNABEL/JUDITH//LAVINIA. Gloom resumes.

DAIMLER. Which isn't to say we should give up all hope.

JUDITH. Whither Hope now?

LAVINIA. Whither the teeniest glimpse?

ANNABEL. Search me.

And CAMILLA *intrudes with a more pressing query.*

CAMILLA. Excuse me, Earth to Mars? Why are we all meanwhile getting changed into our games kit when we don't have a games mistress?

JUDITH. Because we're getting Miss Givings.

CAMILLA (*misunderstanding*). About what? Keeping our clothes on?

JUDITH. No – Miss Givings. She's a temp.

LAVINIA. Probably some awful hefty virgin straight out of teacher-training college.

ANNABEL. Should be here like any mo.

CAMILLA. Please tell me you jest?

ANNABEL/JUDITH//LAVINIA. We don't.

CAMILLA. You mean on top of every other trial and tribulation in this hideous place, we have to chase up and down a damp field in pursuit of a stupid little ball?

JUDITH. We used to love playing hockey, didn't we?

LAVINIA. It used to be *fun*.

ANNABEL. Yeah, like way back in the groove.

CAMILLA. But what's the point of playing it now?

MISS GIVINGS. Survival.

All turn as the immensely dashing MISS GIVINGS *enters – and swoon as she strikes a pose, hockey stick slung over shoulder.*

UPPER SIXTH. Swoon…

Music 5. **Navy Knicks**

MISS GIVINGS.
> **There's a big bad world outside those gates**
> **Not to mention within**
> **A fool is she who hesitates**
> **When her battles begin**
> **I don't mean metaphorically**
> **I'm speaking metabolically**
> **So, get your kit**
> **And let's get fit**
> **To win!**

She whips them into hockey action.

> **Put on your navy knicks**
> **Pick up your hockey sticks**
> **Limber up and watch those muscles grow**

> **Put on your aertex shirts**
> **And those thigh-high pleated skirts**
> **Let's set those rosy cheeks a-glow**

Come on and move your centre forward
Tap your feet and step right back
Every girl should know the score
Good luck to all who come under our attack

Play up and play the field
This team will never yield
One two three bully off and here we go

UPPER SIXTH.
Ground stick, ground stick, ground stick – Go!

Dance routine with hockey sticks.

MISS GIVINGS.
Put on your navy knicks

UPPER SIXTH.
Put on your navy knicks

MISS GIVINGS.
Pick up your hockey sticks

UPPER SIXTH.
Pick up your hockey sticks

MISS GIVINGS.
Prepare to deal the deadly blow

UPPER SIXTH.
We're going to whack that ball into the sky

MISS GIVINGS.
Put on your studded boots

UPPER SIXTH.
Put on your studded boots

MISS GIVINGS.
Cultivate your attributes

UPPER SIXTH.
Cultivate your attributes

MISS GIVINGS.
And if you've got it let it show

UPPER SIXTH.
Line up that goal and let it fly

MISS GIVINGS.
Tackle hard to gain possession

UPPER SIXTH.
Huh! Huh!

MISS GIVINGS.
Fight fiercely if you must

UPPER SIXTH.
Do or die

MISS GIVINGS.
Release your feminine aggression

MISS GIVINGS/UPPER SIXTH.
(And) then move in for the final thrust

MISS GIVINGS.
We know the way to win

UPPER SIXTH.
We know the way to win and how

MISS GIVINGS.
So let the game begin

UPPER SIXTH.
Let's begin right now

MISS GIVINGS.
One two three

MISS GIVINGS/UPPER SIXTH.
Bully off

MISS GIVINGS.
One two three

MISS GIVINGS/UPPER SIXTH.
Bully off

MISS GIVINGS.
One two three

MISS GIVINGS/UPPER SIXTH.
Bully off bully off bully off
And here we go

MISS GIVINGS.
Here we go

MISS GIVINGS/UPPER SIXTH.
Put on your navy knicks
Pick up your hockey sticks
One two three bully off – huh, huh, huh!
One two three bully off – huh, huh, huh!
One two three bully off bully off bully off
And here we go.

All exit, hockey sticks held high.

Music 5a. **Navy Knicks – play-off**

Scene Four

The Head's study.

MISS BLEACHER *is at her desk, gazing at an antique photo frame.*

Knock at door.

She hides the frame in her desk drawer.

MISS BLEACHER. Come!

MISS AUSTIN *enters, carrying a large stack of files.*

MISS AUSTIN. The complete and unabridged personal files of the Upper Sixth, as requested.

MISS BLEACHER. Thank you, Miss Austin.

MISS AUSTIN *sets them down on the edge of the desk.*

MISS AUSTIN. But if I may venture an opinion, Headmistress? About the incident in the art room?

MISS BLEACHER. Venture forth.

MISS AUSTIN. Regrettable though it was, don't you think the sensitivities of the domestic staff would best be mollified by a large tin of Cadbury's Milk Chocolate Assortment?

MISS BLEACHER. What?

MISS AUSTIN. Surely no offence was intended by the two senior girls involved? And is it not the hallowed function of the art room to provide a sanctuary for self-expression?

MISS BLEACHER. Indeed, Miss Austin. That's why I'm eliminating art from the curriculum.

MISS AUSTIN *reels*.

MISS AUSTIN. Eliminating art? But, Headmistress –

Knock at the door.

MISS BLEACHER. Come!

BRENDA *enters*.

Ah, Brenda.

BRENDA. I've got important information about you-know-what, Miss!

MISS BLEACHER. Already? Then divulge it immediately, girl.

BRENDA *is nervous of* MISS AUSTIN.

BRENDA. Um – ?

MISS BLEACHER. In complete confidence, Brenda. Miss Austin and I are equally resolved to close this matter down – are we not, Miss Austin?

MISS AUSTIN (*sighs*). Yes, Headmistress.

MISS BLEACHER. So, Brenda – ?

BRENDA. Well, this time it was going on in the locker room during assembly, Miss.

MISS BLEACHER. For the avoidance of doubt, what was 'going on', Brenda?

BRENDA. Indecent and Unnatural Behaviour, Miss.

MISS BLEACHER. You mean you actually saw it with your own eyes?

BRENDA. Well no, Miss, not exactly. But I definitely heard it with my own ears.

MISS BLEACHER. What? What did you hear?

BRENDA. Kissing, Miss.

MISS BLEACHER. Kissing?

BRENDA. Well, you know, Miss – like this, Miss…

BRENDA *imitates slurpy kissing noises, much to* MISS BLEACHER*'s disgust.*

MISS BLEACHER. Thank you, Brenda. Would you call that evidence, Miss Austin?

MISS AUSTIN. Evidence of something, perhaps – but how can you be sure it was kissing, Brenda?

BRENDA. Because I made a logical deduction, Miss.

MISS AUSTIN. Surely the sounds you have imitated could equally be consistent with the consumption of a cream bun?

MISS BLEACHER. What?

MISS AUSTIN. Which albeit irregular before break would hardly warrant an inquisition?

BRENDA. But I heard words as well, Miss. And I don't think they were about cream buns.

MISS BLEACHER. What words?

BRENDA (*referring to notebook*). 'Oh darling please forgive me you know I love you with all my heart', Miss.

MISS BLEACHER. Well, Miss Austin, I think that's chips for the cream-bun hypothesis, don't you?

MISS AUSTIN. But, Headmistress, some of our girls do use a rather exotic vocabulary.

MISS BLEACHER. Hmm. Are you sure you didn't see anything, Brenda?

BRENDA. I saw enough to recognise who one of them was, Miss.

MISS BLEACHER. Then stop being mysterious. Name her!

BRENDA. Susan Smart, Miss.

MISS BLEACHER. Are you certain?

BRENDA. Oh yes, Miss. I'd swear it on the Bible, Miss.

MISS BLEACHER. Then what about the other girl?

BRENDA. Well, I couldn't swear about *her*, Miss, but I could have a jolly good guess.

MISS AUSTIN. Ahem. I don't think the suppositions of the witness can be counted as evidence, Headmistress.

MISS BLEACHER. Are you absolutely sure you can't be sure, Brenda?

BRENDA. I'm sorry, Miss.

MISS BLEACHER. Very well. Leave this with us and hurry along with your other task.

BRENDA. I came in early to clear out the art room, Miss. And I've compiled a tabulated inventory of all equipment in transit, so I can cross-check each item on and off my trolley, Miss.

MISS BLEACHER. Very diligent, Brenda. If you fail to find a husband, I'm sure you'll be a great asset to the Inland Revenue.

BRENDA. Yes, Miss. Thank you, Miss!

She exits.

MISS BLEACHER *crows.*

MISS BLEACHER. So – we have a name!

MISS AUSTIN. But Susan Smart is one of our shining lights, Headmistress. To be nurtured and cherished.

MISS BLEACHER. Oh really, Miss Austin, you don't seem to grasp the moral exigency here. Two reports in as many days, in separate locations? If we don't root out this vile canker it could spread round the whole school.

MISS AUSTIN (*resigned nod*). Yes, Headmistress, you're quite right...

MISS BLEACHER. Then let us wield the scalpel!

MISS AUSTIN. No, I mean you're quite right I don't grasp your point. And forgive me, but did we not fight the last war to defeat fascism?

A beat. MISS BLEACHER *ponders this challenge.*

MISS BLEACHER. What are you saying, Miss Austin? That we shouldn't teach our girls to become good wives and mothers?

MISS AUSTIN. Not at all, Headmistress, if they so aspire. Indeed I once hoped to become one myself. But my family were thankful when my fiancé was killed in action – because they couldn't bear *their* daughter to be the first GI bride in Dorking.

MISS BLEACHER *grimaces.*

A fact I only disclose, Headmistress, by way of broadening the argument –

But by way of her expansive gesture, the pile of files is sent flying.

Oops!

MISS BLEACHER *ends all further argument.*

MISS BLEACHER. Kindly clear up your mess before I return, Miss Austin. I have an urgent letter to dictate.

MISS AUSTIN. Yes, Headmistress.

MISS BLEACHER *exits, leaving* MISS AUSTIN *to pick up the pieces.*

Oh dear, poor Susan. How many more battles have we yet to win?

Music 6. **A Young Heart**

> **A young heart**
> **And a young mind**
> **Still believing**
> **That the world is kind**
> **And still not**
> **Disillusioned with love**
>
> **A light step**
> **With a light head**
> **Flitting madly**
> **Where your heart is led**
> **And lost in**
> **The confusion of love**
>
> **No cares on your shoulder**
> **Just a feeling the world's at your feet**
> **Who cares when you're older**
> **Live the moment and life will be sweet**
>
> **Keep a young heart**
> **And a young mind**
> **If you search hard**
> **You will find**
> **You're still not**
> **Disillusioned**
> **You're still lost**
> **In confusion**
> **And I'm still not**
> **Disillusioned with love.**

Sounds off of a pane of glass smashing. A whistle blows.

Oh! They really are playing hockey again!

MISS GIVINGS (*off*). Short corner!

MISS AUSTIN. Wait for me!

Music 6a. **A Young Heart – play-off**

She dumps the files on the desk and dashes out.

Scene Five

Locker room.

SUSAN *and* CAMILLA *return from hockey practice –* CAMILLA *wearing goalie's pads and covered in mud, limping on hockey-stick crutches.*

CAMILLA. Hockey isn't a game, it's a blood sport. Ow!

SUSAN. Poor darling.

CAMILLA. I thought Miss Givings put me in goal for ornamental purposes, not to be set upon by that horde of marauding Amazons.

SUSAN. But you did pull off a spectacular save when you dived for cover.

CAMILLA. Oh, just get these great chunks off my legs and give me a massage.

CAMILLA *sits and* SUSAN *kneels before her, to remove pads and commence leg massage – as* JUDITH, LAVINIA, ANNABEL *and* MISS AUSTIN *enter with hockey sticks, muddy and exhausted but in high spirits.*

MISS AUSTIN. I'm so proud of you, dear girls. We've got our team spirit back.

JUDITH. Your stick work was simply stunning, Miss Austin.

ANNABEL. Like outta sight, man!

LAVINIA. You had the whole school cheering us out of the windows.

MISS AUSTIN. All bar one… (*Conspiratorial whisper.*) Who I'm dismayed to report is not only being deployed as the Despot's eyes and ears, but also as her arms and legs…

The trio lean in to hear the rest.

…Brenda Smears…

The trio reel.

ANNABEL/JUDITH//LAVINIA. Gasp!

MISS AUSTIN. So I must urge you to tackle *her.*

JUDITH. Will do.

LAVINIA. D'accord.

ANNABEL. Dig.

MISS AUSTIN. And I must convey my gratitude to our new champion, Miss Givings. Who, unless my memory has been utterly unhinged by vain hope, bears a striking resemblance to one of our old girls…

The trio query, but MISS AUSTIN *makes her exit.*

See you in the refectory at break – the orange slices are on me.

The trio take towels and exit to the showers, all abuzz with intrigue. Meanwhile CAMILLA *is reassessing her muddied arms as* SUSAN *massages her legs.*

CAMILLA. Actually, mud's rather good for you, isn't it? My mother pays a fortune for this at her spa.

SUSAN. May I have the other leg, madam?

CAMILLA. You may. But nothing could induce me into those disgusting cold showers. I'd sooner take a dip in the duck pond.

SUSAN. Tell me where it hurts.

CAMILLA. Down a bit – there! Ah…

CAMILLA *abandons herself to* SUSAN*'s ministrations – as* BENNY *enters, backwards, checking no one's on his tail – then turns around and jolts.*

BENNY. Uh – sorry – sorry –

SUSAN *and* CAMILLA *jolt apart –* BENNY *shields his eyes – and* CAMILLA *is captivated.*

CAMILLA. Well, hello… Who are *you*?

BENNY. Uh – Benny. Benny the Bag. Odd-job man.

CAMILLA. Really? And what odd job may we ask do you propose to do for us?

BENNY. Uh – nah – nah – I'll come back laters – sorry – awright –

He makes an over-hasty retreat, as CAMILLA *tries to caution –*

CAMILLA. Um – that's actually the way to the girls' –

Chorus of screams off.

– showers…

BENNY *spins back in, all the more flustered, and bolts for the exit.*

Don't dash, I'm sure we can think of something –

He's gone. She sighs.

What a dish! I think I'm in love.

SUSAN. Oh, darling, don't try and make me jealous, I can't bear it.

CAMILLA. You dear little green thing, I tease. As if I could ever fall for such excruciating vowels!

SUSAN. Comme je t'adore, ma reine!

CAMILLA. Comme tu dois, mon esclave.

They embrace – as DAIMLER *enters in high spirits.*

DAIMLER.
We're going to whack that ball into the sky –

She stiffens to see them jolt apart.

Eggy beat.

SUSAN. Daimler!

DAIMLER. Fortunately for you. Found the penalty ball too.

She waves a hockey ball – then turns aside to her locker.

Don't worry, I'm not stopping.

CAMILLA. Neither are we. Fetch our things, Susan. We're going to sneak back to the dorm and luxuriate in a hot bath.

SUSAN. Darling!

CAMILLA *exits, leaving* SUSAN *to grab their clothes.*

Be divine and cover for us, Daimler? If we're late back for Latin?

DAIMLER. Why ask me? As if I'd care if you get expelled and ruin your entire life.

SUSAN. Oh, darling, of course you care. You're my best friend in the whole universe.

DAIMLER. Yes. I'm a little speck surrounded by a whole load of nothing.

SUSAN. Oh, silly, you're my absolute rock. I wouldn't know what to do if I didn't have you to talk to.

DAIMLER. Then why don't you listen to me?

SUSAN. But I do! Every poem I've ever written to Camilla I've asked your advice.

DAIMLER. Oh God, you make me so mad!

SUSAN. But it's true!

DAIMLER. Oh just go.

Awkward beat.

Then SUSAN *rushes off.*

And DAIMLER *slumps.*

Music 7. **Too Much in Love**

**So here I am again
The one who's left behind
I may be her best friend
But I'm the last thing on her mind**

**I know she doesn't see
Any more to me than – me
Any moment she can spare
I'm her soulmate who will share
Every book that she's read
Every thought in her head
Oh but she's too much in love
To think of me**

On me she can depend
'Good old Daimler', till the end
Always close at hand
So prepared to understand
I'm a great confidante
But that's not what I want
Oh but she's too much in love
To think of me

She says Camilla
Can fill her
With a passion that could kill her
And I listen so patiently
But I want to take her
And shake her
And somehow try to make her
Feel the same for me

But instead I don't let it show
When I can't bear her to go
I keep it inside
Well there's a small matter of pride
Maybe I should leave her be
If I could then I'd be free
Oh but I'm too much in love
To think about me
Oh but I'm too much in love
To think about me.

She puts her head in her hands – as a preoccupied MISS
GIVINGS *enters, checking her watch, then is pulled up to
find this unexpected obstacle to her own plans.*

But duty evidently calls…

She makes a little cough.

MISS GIVINGS. Enter Miss Givings.

DAIMLER *startles.*

Trying not to startle you.

DAIMLER *flusters.*

DAIMLER. I – I seem to have misplaced my towel…

MISS GIVINGS produces a handkerchief.

MISS GIVINGS. Here – use this.

DAIMLER takes it and blows her nose.

DAIMLER. Sorry. I'm just a bit down in the dumps.

MISS GIVINGS. So what's whacked you in the shins, then?

DAIMLER. Oh, nothing. Everything. Oh, it's just all completely hopeless.

MISS GIVINGS. Right… Well, I can't give you a plaster for internal injuries, kid. But I can give you my word the game's not over yet – and now is not the time to give up the fight, if you want to help Miss Austin save this school?

DAIMLER looks up.

So – better chin up and get back on the team, hey?

DAIMLER grits her teeth and rallies.

DAIMLER. Well, even if I can't win, Miss, I jolly well know what I'm fighting for.

MISS GIVINGS. That's the spirit!

She heads DAIMLER off to the showers, then lights up a cigarette and breathes relief – as a wary BENNY creeps in behind her back, then turns to see her – and smirks.

BENNY. Ooh, dodgy habit for a games mistress, Miss.

She startles, then snaps back at him in her true persona.

DIANA. Not as dodgy as your ridiculous accent.

BENNY. Eh? Dontcha know yours truly was famed for me Eliza Doolittle in the Footlights?

DIANA. Oh, do grow up, Dorian. Your career at Cambridge was only famed for the glittering speed at which you got sent down.

DORIAN drops his BENNY act.

DORIAN. All right, bossy big sis, but I haven't been entirely useless gathering proof that Bleacher's got to go. Wait till you hear what I taped in assembly – her values are positively Victorian!

DIANA. Luckily the Dosserdalian spirit is still in formidable form on the hockey pitch. And I knew we'd have a trusty ally in dear Miss Austin. But she fears it's only a matter of days before Bleacher forces her into retirement.

DORIAN. Then all we need is for the tiresome lawyers to grant you sole Governorship pro tem in extremis, as per Sub-Clause Twenty-Three – (*Holds up his bag.*) sufficient cause QED!

DIANA. So we need you to persuade them to pull their fingers out, Dorian.

DORIAN. Me? Um – how?

DIANA. You went to school with the senior partner's tiresome son, didn't you? So oil the wheels as old boys traditionally do.

DORIAN. You mean – you want me to wine and dine the deadly boring Percy Puttifoot?

DIANA. Drive up to town tomorrow, go to work in your darkroom, deliver all the evidence to his office. Then take him to The Ritz and twist his arm, so we can liberate these poor kids by Friday.

DORIAN (*sighs*). Right. Fine. But, oh God, it's so tedious having to stand up and fight for things.

School bell rings.

DIANA. Get some snaps of the library and art room. Then meet me back at The Pig and Whistle.

They exit separately.

Music 7a. **Prepare to Pounce**

Scene Six

Main lobby.

JUDITH, LAVINIA *and* ANNABEL *enter stealthily, on their mission to tackle* BRENDA.

ANNABEL. Here comes the creep!

JUDITH. Right, prepare to pounce.

> BRENDA *enters, pushing a trolley laden with science equipment. The trio leap out to block her path every which way – and* BRENDA *is alarmed to find herself trapped.*

BRENDA. What are you doing? Is this one of your pranks?

JUDITH. We think it's time you explained what *you're* doing, Brenda.

BRENDA. I'm on special orders from Miss Bleacher to take this science equipment up to the art room, obviously. Which means if you don't get out of my way I'll report you.

JUDITH. But Dosserdalians don't blindly carry out orders, Brenda.

LAVINIA. Our founder would call that collaborating with the enemy.

ANNABEL. And we ain't hip to that, dig?

BRENDA. Well, for your information our founder was deluded. Because hard work and discipline will shape our destiny, not so-called 'free-thinking'. And I say hip-hip-hoorah!

> *The others exchange appalled looks.*

JUDITH. She's been totally brainwashed –

LAVINIA. To be a sneak and a toady with no shame –

ANNABEL. Like worse than square, she's cubed!

BRENDA. You boarders think you can look down on me just because I'm a day bug, don't you?

JUDITH. Oh, don't be silly. It's not because you're a day bug –

ANNABEL. It's cos you're *you*!

LAVINIA. Any decent Dosserdalian girl would dump that trolley and skive off to sick bay with a 'sprained ankle'.

BRENDA. Well, for your further information, you'll be expelled for that sort of showy-offy disobedience in future. And it serves you right!

JUDITH. Oh, Brenda, why do you persist in being so beastly?

LAVINIA. Do you want us all to hate you?

BRENDA. You've always hated me. Ever since I was in the preps.

JUDITH. But that's not true – (*Bemused aside to the others.*) Was she in the preps?

Blank looks and shrugs.

ANNABEL. Like – duh?

LAVINIA. We barely noticed her at all until she turned traitor for Bleacher – did we?

And BRENDA *scorns them all from the depths of her wounded heart.*

BRENDA. You see! You've no idea how horrible you've been to me, have you?

Music 8. **It's Not Fair**

I am that worm on which the whole world treads
Whom not even God can see
I've never been behind the bicycle sheds
No one shares their sweets with me

ANNABEL/JUDITH/LAVINIA. But that's *your* fault!

BRENDA.
I can't help being good at trigonometry
It's just the way I was born
I'm tired of everybody going on at me
It's clear I'm an object of scorn
It's not my fault that I'm the best

At Venn diagrams and graphs
But every time there's a science test
And I come top everybody laughs
It's not fair

ANNABEL/JUDITH/LAVINIA.
'Snot, 'snot, it's not fair

BRENDA.
It's not fair

ANNABEL/JUDITH/LAVINIA.
'Snot, 'snot, it's not fair

BRENDA.
I can't help being rubbish on the hockey pitch
I just can't run very fast

ANNABEL/JUDITH/LAVINIA.
She just can't run very fast

BRENDA.
I'm looking at my feet and wondering which is which
Meanwhile the ball has gone past
It's not my fault that I'm shortsighted
And I haven't got perfect teeth

ANNABEL/JUDITH/LAVINIA.
She is not to blame
For shame
Aaah – aahh

BRENDA.
With frizzy hair I know I'm blighted
But I've still got feelings underneath

ANNABEL/JUDITH/LAVINIA.
Ooh, wah-ooh

BRENDA.
You think that you're so decent
But you haven't a clue

ANNABEL/JUDITH/LAVINIA.
Wah-wah-wah-ooh, wah-ooh-ooh

BRENDA.
    What life is really like
    For someone not as lucky as you
    So what if I'm stuck in a laboratory

ANNABEL/JUDITH/LAVINIA.
        Na-na-na, na-na-na

BRENDA.
    Where everything is pickled and dead

ANNABEL/JUDITH/LAVINIA.
        Na-na-na-na-na-na-na

BRENDA.
    But that's the only way to get a science degree

ANNABEL/JUDITH/LAVINIA.
        Na-na-na, na-na-na

BRENDA.
    And forge my own future ahead

ANNABEL/JUDITH/LAVINIA.
        Na-na-na-na-na-na-na

BRENDA.
    And just because I am not like you

ANNABEL/JUDITH/LAVINIA.
        Aah-aah, aah-aah

BRENDA.
    Doesn't mean my life is wrong
    But you've always mocked everything I do

ANNABEL/JUDITH/LAVINIA.
        Aah-aah, aah-aah

BRENDA.
    And made me feel like I don't belong

ANNABEL/JUDITH/LAVINIA.
        That's not fair!

BRENDA (*mocking them back*).
    Yeah? Yeah? Yeah, yeah!

ANNABEL/JUDITH/LAVINIA.
> That's not fair

BRENDA.
> Yeah? Yeah! It's not fair!

> Can't throw, can't catch, can't shoot

ANNABEL/JUDITH/LAVINIA.
> > Can't win, can't play, can't cope

BRENDA.
> I'm always substitute
> Can't act, can't sing, can't dance

ANNABEL/JUDITH/LAVINIA.
> > She's got no hope!

BRENDA.
> I don't have any chance

ANNABEL/JUDITH/LAVINIA.
> > > And it's not fair –
> > > It's not fair –
> > > It's not fair –
> > > It's not fair –

BRENDA.
> I've always been excluded
> But one day you will regret what you did
> And you'll be sad but I won't care
> Whoa-oh, whoa, it's not fair

ANNABEL/JUDITH/LAVINIA.
> > > Na-na-na-na-na it's not fair
> > > It's not fair
> > > Na-na-na-na-na it's not fair... (*Repeat.*)

BRENDA.
> It's not fair, it's not fair
> Na-na-na-na no it's not fair
> 'Snot, 'snot, 'snot, it's not fair!
> So there!

> BRENDA *bolts off with the trolley, leaving the defeated trio in a spin.*

JUDITH (*sighs*). We'll have to try another tack.

They exit.

Music 8a. **'Snot Fair – play-off**

Scene Seven

The Headmistress's study.

It's empty and the desk is clear.

Knock at the door.

Then another knock.

Then BRENDA *puts her head round the door.*

BRENDA. Miss?

She sidles in, and within seconds is compulsively taking a snoop in the desk drawer – to find the photo frame and to puzzle... And she only just covers her tracks before MISS BLEACHER *enters, carrying an envelope.*

MISS BLEACHER. Ah, Brenda. Mission accomplished?

BRENDA. Yes, Miss. The art room's now fully equipped as science room two and all the art equipment's in the cellar awaiting shipment to the poor primitive children in Africa.

MISS BLEACHER. Excellent.

BRENDA. But it wasn't easy or enjoyable, Miss. I did have to escape an ambush and defend my integrity.

MISS BLEACHER. Well, don't bleat about it, girl. Opposition is the engine of endeavour.

BRENDA. Yes, Miss.

MISS BLEACHER. So here's your next task, Brenda – if I can entrust it to your utmost stealth and secrecy?

BRENDA. On my honour or hope to die, Miss!

MISS BLEACHER. Then take this to the post office straight after school and have it sent 'special delivery'.

MISS BLEACHER *gives her the envelope – and* BRENDA *glints as she reads the address.*

BRENDA. To Susan Smart's parents?

MISS BLEACHER. Thanks to your dogged fieldwork, Brenda, as of tomorrow morning I shall truly turn the tide in this school. And you will be rewarded with the honour of being my Head Girl.

BRENDA. Gosh, Miss… Jubilate!

She scurries out.

MISS BLEACHER *retrieves the photo frame from the desk drawer and gazes at it, with messianic zeal.*

MISS BLEACHER. Thy will *will* be done…

Music 8b. **Future Mothers – reprise**

> **We strive to educate**
> **So you may better procreate**
> **And that henceforth shall be –**
> **The function of this school**
> **The function of this school…**

She exits.

Transition to next morning:

Scene Eight

Sixth-form dorm corridor – Thursday morning.

JUDITH, ANNABEL, LAVINIA, DAIMLER, CAMILLA
and SUSAN *line up for the bathroom, with dressing gowns and
bath bags.*

JUDITH. Once more unto the beastly breach, dear friends.

ANNABEL/CAMILLA/LAVINIA/SUSAN. Groan!

DAIMLER. Oh, buck up, you lot. Let's at least put on a brave
face.

> BRENDA *enters, in uniform, all smug officiousness.*
> CAMILLA *recoils, shielding her eyes.*

CAMILLA. Eurgh!

BRENDA. Message for Susan Smart. Matron says to come to
her office immediately.

SUSAN. Me? Why, what for?

BRENDA. Because your parents are on the phone saying they
urgently need to speak to you.

> *She exits, leaving consternation in her wake.*

SUSAN. My parents?

JUDITH. Bad news or what?

LAVINIA. Quoi d'autre?

ANNABEL. Death or disaster for deffo.

DAIMLER. Oh, don't be so negative!

SUSAN. But it must be something serious, mustn't it?

> DAIMLER *can't disagree. But* CAMILLA *has a brainwave.*

CAMILLA. Or it could be something ultra-fabulous, Susan…

SUSAN. Like what?

CAMILLA. Perhaps they've won the football pools and you're
going to be as rich as I am!

SUSAN. What?

CAMILLA. They live in a council house, don't they? Surely they must *do* them?

SUSAN. Well, yes, but –

CAMILLA. Well, dash along and find out!

They exit to bathroom, leaving SUSAN *to face the music with her parents in a stylised sequence.*

Music 9. **It's Only Because We Love You**

SUSAN. Hello? Mum? Dad?

MUM. Indecent?

DAD. Unnatural?

MUM. Depraved? Oh, Susan –

Is this really the way you behaved?

SUSAN. What?

MUM. It says here in this letter.

DAD. From your Headmistress –

MUM.
Though I'm sure it can't be true

SUSAN. What?

MUM.
**That you and another girl were –
Seen...**

DAD.
**I think perhaps we'd better
Hear the rest of it from you
Are you now or have you ever – been...?**

You know what we mean –

MUM.
**It's only because we love you
Only because we care**

DAD.

> **We just want the truth**
> **Now tell us the truth**

MUM.

> **Your problems are problems to share**

SUSAN. I can't believe this is happening!

MUM.

> **Whatever's wrong we'll understand**

DAD.

> **Somebody must be lying**

MUM.

> **It's just a story second-hand**

DAD/MUM.

> **That only needs denying darling**
> **Tell us now it can't be true!**

DAD. So come on. Are you innocent or guilty?

> MUM *restrains* DAD.

MUM. Susan?

SUSAN.

> **I've done nothing to be made ashamed for**
> **There is nothing that I could be blamed for**
> **Why should I have to deny it?**
> **There's no reason...**

MUM. There! I knew it was all a mistake.

DAD. No, just a minute – you *mean* something, don't you?

SUSAN.

> **I was kissing the girl that I love...**

> MUM *and* DAD *recoil*.

> **And that's entirely natural**
> **And entirely decent too**
> **And it isn't in the very least depraved**

MUM.

> Oh God, I don't believe it
> Look we'll say it wasn't you

DAD/MUM.

> Susan you must be saved!

SUSAN. Leave me alone!

DAD/MUM.

> It's only because we love you
> We have to set you straight
> We'll get you the best
> Whatever is best

DAD.

> I hope that it isn't too late

MUM.

> What have we done to let you down?
> Maybe you feel neglected?

DAD.

> Oh come on don't let's mess around
> It's nothing we hadn't suspected

DAD/MUM.

> We only ever want to make you happy
> We know a doctor who could make you happy
> Let him help us help you make us happy Susan...

SUSAN. You mean you want to send me to a psychiatrist?

DAD/MUM.

> It's only because we love you
> Only for your own good
> Whatever we do
> We do it for you

MUM.

> Though often we're misunderstood
> One day you're going to thank us dear

DAD.

> One day you will be grateful
> I hope I make myself quite clear

MUM.
> **It's not that we're trying to be hateful**

SUSAN. But you are!

DAD/MUM.
> **It's only because we love you**

SUSAN. No you don't!

MUM.
> **Only because we love you...**

DAD. We're going to put a stop to this, Susan.

DAD/MUM.
> **It's only because we love you**
> **And because... we... care...**

> MUM *and* DAD *disappear, leaving* SUSAN *in shock – to be rejoined by the* UPPER SIXTH *boarders, all now in uniform.*

JUDITH. Well?

LAVINIA. Qu'est-ce qu'ils ont dit?

ANNABEL. Spill the beans!

CAMILLA. Are they upgrading to a Rolls or a Bentley?

> DAIMLER *detects all is not well.*

DAIMLER. Susan – ?

SUSAN. Bleacher's written to my parents saying I'm guilty of Indecent and Unnatural Behaviour...

ALL. Gasp?

SUSAN. And if I don't confess and name who with then I'm going to be expelled...

ALL. Gasp??

SUSAN. And my parents are on her side!

ALL. Gasp???!!

SUSAN (*to* CAMILLA). But I swear I'll never divulge your name, darling, whatever tortures they inflict on me.

CAMILLA. Oh, don't get in a stew. There's only one thing to do now.

SUSAN. What?

CAMILLA. Run away to London, of course! And I'm coming with you.

SUSAN. But, darling – you can't – or you'll get expelled too.

CAMILLA. No, I'll just bribe Matron to say she's sent me home with scarlet fever. And trust my mother to provide backup.

School bell rings.

You pack our cases, I'll meet you outside.

She dashes out.

JUDITH. We'll tell Miss Austin and try and cover for you at roll-call.

The trio dash out.

DAIMLER. But you can't just give up and go, Susan.

That's what Bleacher wants, isn't it?

SUSAN. I've got no choice, have I?

DAIMLER. But –

SUSAN *exits – leaving* DAIMLER *in a stew.*

Scene Nine

The school quad.

JUDITH, LAVINIA *and* ANNABEL *are in a huddle with* MISS AUSTIN – *to be joined by* DAIMLER.

MISS AUSTIN. Oh no... Oh, poor Susan... Oh, goodness me...

MISS BLEACHER *enters and grimaces.*

MISS BLEACHER. What are you all doing in a huddle? Didn't you hear the bell for roll-call? Line them up for inspection, Miss Austin!

MISS AUSTIN *promptly spreads her arms wide to guard the* GIRLS *and ward off their foe.*

MISS AUSTIN. I'm sorry, Headmistress, but in my capacity as Senior First Aider I must advise you to stand back and cover your mouth.

MISS BLEACHER. What?

MISS AUSTIN. There's been a sudden outbreak of suspected scarlet fever in the sixth-form dorm.

The UPPER SIXTH *take the hint and start coughing and groaning.*

MISS BLEACHER. What?

MISS AUSTIN. Matron's already had to send Camilla Faraday home with symptoms. And I'm taking the precaution of quarantining her dorm mates in sick bay.

She tries to flurry them off, but MISS BLEACHER*'s counting heads.*

MISS BLEACHER. Just a minute... And what ails Susan Smart? Bubonic plague?

MISS AUSTIN. Um – sorry, Headmistress, I assumed you knew. Susan had to take an urgent telephone call from her parents.

MISS BLEACHER. Then you should also have assumed I knew precisely when and what about, Miss Austin.

BRENDA *rushes in.*

BRENDA. Excuse me, Miss, but I've just acted on my own initiative to go on a recce in the sixth-form dorm – and Susan Smart's suitcase is missing with all of her things!

MISS AUSTIN and GIRLS grimace, MISS BLEACHER glints.

MISS BLEACHER. Guilty as charged!

MISS AUSTIN. But, Headmistress –

MISS BLEACHER. As are you all. Whole-school detention, assembly hall, now!

Music 10. **Run Away / Stay**

Ring the bell, Brenda.

BRENDA. Yes, Miss!

BRENDA skips off, MISS BLEACHER herds out the others.

Then SUSAN sneaks in, wearing uniform, with two suitcases.

SUSAN. Camilla – ? Are you here?

CAMILLA emerges from her hiding place.

CAMILLA. Poised for departure, Susan. Complete with drab disguise via the staff cloakroom to ward off lewd lorry drivers en route.

She produces two overcoats.

SUSAN. Why, what are we disguised as? Dirty old men?

CAMILLA. Jehovah's Witnesses!

SUSAN. Darling, you think of everything!

School bell rings with extra vigour.

CAMILLA.
> **When there's no doubt**
> **You have been found out**
> **Run, run away**
> **When you come adrift**
> **Go out and thumb a lift**
> **And make your getaway**

SUSAN.
> **When discipline**
> **Hits you on the chin**
> **Don't take it like a man**
> **Why don't you just let rip**
> **That stiff upper lip**
> **And run as fast as you can?**

CAMILLA/SUSAN.
> **We're in dead lumber**
> **If we ever go back**
> **They've got our number**
> **The enemy is on the attack**
>
> **So when you're overpowered**
> **Why not be a coward**
> **And keep your head down**
> **Why stay and fight**
> **When you could take flight**
> **And wing your way out of town?**

Transition to:

Assembly hall.

MISS BLEACHER *taps out lines written on blackboard for the guilty to intone and* BRENDA *to relish.*

MISS BLEACHER/MISS AUSTIN/UPPER SIXTH.
> **To – conceal – a – sin – is – to – share – the – guilt**
> **Disce aut discede!**
> **To – conceal – a – sin – is – to – share – the – guilt**
> **Learn or depart!**
> **To – conceal – a – sin – is – to – share – the – guilt –**
> (*Etc.*)

The chant continues under the verse, as SUSAN *and* CAMILLA *sneak on their way.*

CAMILLA/SUSAN.
> **Why face the music**
> **When they are calling the tune?**
> **Darling, if you stick**
> **With me we'll be immune**

I say enough's enough
Why should we play it tough?
We're too young to die
When the chips are down
Why pull an ugly frown?
Just smile and wave bye-bye.

Transition to:

School gates.

SUSAN *spins with excited anticipation.*

SUSAN. We'll pay homage to the statue of Eros, then go in search of that secret nightclub in Chelsea!

But CAMILLA*'s thoughts are elsewhere.*

CAMILLA. Sunglasses…

SUSAN. No, it was called The Stairways, wasn't it?

CAMILLA*'s rooting through her suitcase.*

CAMILLA. What?

SUSAN. You know, where your mother said she danced with Marlene Dietrich when she was an art student?

CAMILLA. I'm saying where are my sunglasses, Susan? You did pack them, didn't you?

SUSAN*'s face falls.*

I can't face the elements without them, can I? Nor complete our disguise.

SUSAN. I'll run back and get them.

CAMILLA. No, I'll run back. You wait in the bushes.

She sprints off and SUSAN *scurries into hiding with the suitcases.*

The DOSSERDALES *enter –* DIANA *in* 'MISS GIVINGS' *disguise,* DORIAN *as himself in trendy casuals – to run through checklist for his departure.*

DIANA. Kitbag, case notes, keys to Chelsea flat.

DORIAN. Check.

DIANA. Keep your mind on your mission, I'll rustle up a petition.

DORIAN. Roger that, wish me luck, chocks off, over and out.

He dashes off and she shouts after him.

DIANA. And that means no distractions, Dorian!

DORIAN (*waving her a thumb-up*). Piccadilly, here I come!

DIANA *sprints away into school – and* DAIMLER *rushes out, looking this way and that.*

DAIMLER. Susan? Susan, where are you? Oh, for goodness' sake...

Why don't you stay?
Running away is just a delay
You'll still have to brave it and face it some day
Why don't you stand up and face it today?
Show them the way –

SUSAN *emerges from the bushes.*

SUSAN. I know you think I'm being a worm, Daimler, but even Oscar Wilde wasn't put on trial when he was still at school, was he?

DAIMLER. If Oscar Wilde had run away from his persecutors, Susan, he would never have written 'The Ballad of Reading Gaol' or 'De Profundis'.

SUSAN *is confounded.*

SUSAN. Oh, why do you always do this to me?

DAIMLER. Do what? Make you think a bit harder about what you really value?

SUSAN *is struck by* DAIMLER*'s intensity, but they're jolted apart as* CAMILLA *rushes in.*

CAMILLA. Susan?

SUSAN. Darling –

CAMILLA *stiffens to see* DAIMLER.

CAMILLA. What's *she* doing here? Waving us off?

SUSAN. Daimler thinks we should stay and fight to save the school.

CAMILLA. We're fighting to save our love, Susan. And we're doing it in style.

She produces two pairs of sunglasses.

(*To* SUSAN). Me Pucci, you Gucci!

They don glasses and pose – and DAIMLER *despairs as* SUSAN *falls back under* CAMILLA*'s spell.*

>When there's no doubt
>You have been found out
>Run, run away

CAMILLA/SUSAN.
>When you come adrift
>Go out and thumb a lift
>And make your getaway

DAIMLER.
>Why don't you listen to a word that I say?

CAMILLA/SUSAN.
>We're in dead lumber
>If we ever go back
>They've got our
>   number
>The enemy is on the
>   attack
>So when you're
>   overpowered
>Why not be a coward
>And keep your head
>   down?
>Why stay and fight
>When you could take
>   flight
>And wing your way
>   out of town?

DAIMLER.
>Running away is just a
>   delay
>You'll still have to
>   brave it and face it
>   some day
>Why don't you stand
>   up and face it
>   today?
>Show them the way
>And stay
>Stay
>Don't leave me this
>   way
>Stay
>Please!

DAIMLER.
>Why don't you listen to a word that I say?

CAMILLA.

Why face the music?

SUSAN.

We'll go far, far from here

DAIMLER.

Running away is just a delay

CAMILLA.

When they are calling the tune

SUSAN.

To be who we are

DAIMLER.

You'll still have to brave it and face it some day

CAMILLA.

Darling if you stick

SUSAN.

With nothing to fear

DAIMLER.

So why don't you stand up and face it today?

CAMILLA.

With me we'll be immune

DAIMLER.

Show them the way
And stay

CAMILLA.

I say enough's enough

SUSAN.

For liberty

DAIMLER.

Stay

CAMILLA.

Why should we play it tough?

SUSAN.

For poetry

DAIMLER.
> **Don't leave me this way**

CAMILLA.
> **We're too young to die**

SUSAN.
> **For everything I long to be**

CAMILLA.
> **When the chips are down**

SUSAN.
> **For love and truth**

DAIMLER.
> **Stay**

CAMILLA.
> **Why pull an ugly frown**

SUSAN.
> **For reckless youth**

DAIMLER.
> **Please, stay**

CAMILLA.
> **Just smile and wave bye-bye**

SUSAN.
> **I'll make them rue this day**

Sound of a lorry horn: TOOT-TOOT!

Look, a lorry!

SUSAN and CAMILLA look in its direction, then at each other.

CAMILLA.
> **It's a total non-starter**
> **To be a martyr…**

SUSAN. Piccadilly, here we come!

They pick up their cases to run for the lorry.

CAMILLA/SUSAN.
Run run run run run
Run away –

Final tableau with all factions.

MISS BLEACHER/UPPER SIXTH.
Disce aut discede

DAIMLER.
Stay –

MISS AUSTIN/MISS GIVINGS/DORIAN.
Save our school!

CAMILLA/SUSAN.
Run away –

DAIMLER.
Stay –

MISS AUSTIN/MISS GIVINGS/DORIAN.
Save our school!

CAMILLA/SUSAN.
Run away!

MISS BLEACHER/UPPER SIXTH.
Disce aut discede

DAIMLER.
Stay!

MISS AUSTIN/MISS GIVINGS/DORIAN.
Save our school!

SUSAN *and* CAMILLA *make their escape, leaving*
DAIMLER *in dismay and the school in disarray.*

End of Act One.

ACT TWO

Scene Ten

Piccadilly Circus – Thursday evening.

Music 11. **Hello London!**

A cacophony of traffic, crowds, and a dazzle of bright lights.

SUSAN *and* CAMILLA *rush in, in disguise and with cases.*

CAMILLA.
> **Hello London!**

SUSAN.
> **Hello Piccadilly!**

CAMILLA.
> **How absolutely thrilly to be here amidst the throng**

CAMILLA/SUSAN.
> **To feel that we're a part of it**
> **Inside the beating heart of it**
> **Eros hear our song**
> **London is where we belong**
>
> **With fellow rebels**
> **Vagabonds and poets**
> **In Soho don't you know it's so bohemian and free**
> **We'll rove around Fitzrovia**
> **That arty treasure trovia**
> **In a room in Bloomsbury**
> **We'll commune with the Literati**
>
> **No more putting up with petty-minded rules**
> **We are true free spirits from now on**
> **Half the trick to matric is simply getting out of school**
> **So goodbye to all that and be gone**
>
> **Hurrah for London**
> **Hip-hip Piccadilly**

> **Finally our brilliant adventure has begun**
> **Now all of life begins again**
> **The wheel of fortune spins again**
> **See how far we've spun**
> **We have made it to Double-u One!**

SUSAN looks in her purse with dismay.

SUSAN. But how do we make it to SW3 with only tuppence ha'penny left in the kitty?

CAMILLA. Oh, drat! I forgot about the tedious necessities. I'll get my mother to wire us some first thing tomorrow. And we'll just have to bear our cross tonight and do as needs must.

SUSAN. What?

CAMILLA. Follow moi.

They take their suitcases aside – as DORIAN enters, wearing formal evening wear, despatching his inebriated companion (Percy Puttifoot) in a black cab.

DORIAN. Albany. Keep the change.

He waves the cab away.

Worth every penny, Percy old chum!

He sighs with relief, job done – and relishes his freedom to have fun.

> **No more listening to boring legalese**
> **I have done my duty for the cause**
> **Now there's half an evening to do with as I please**
> **And again I remain most faithfully yours**
>
> **Dearest London**
> **Dear old Piccadilly**
> **Call me silly but I really must confess**
> **There's nowhere else I'd rather be**
> **Cupid aim your dart at me**
> **I'll always say yes**
> **London's my favourite address.**

CAMILLA and SUSAN return to set up their pitch – CAMILLA with red lipsticked placard: 'TO GIVE IS

DIVINE', SUSAN with crucifix made from wooden ruler, comb and elastic bands, rattling coins in an enamel tooth mug.

CAMILLA. The Lord sayeth blessed are the poor! So give us thy pennies or thou shalt surely go to Hell!

PASSERS-BY give them a wide berth – but DORIAN's intrigued and makes a beeline.

The end is nigh! Help a pauper before you die!

DORIAN. Let me guess your sect. Something seriously Armageddony, right?

CAMILLA. Sorry?

DORIAN. Seventh Day Adventists? Mormons?

CAMILLA. Oh, you mean –

SUSAN. We're Jehovah's Witnesses.

DORIAN. Yikes!

CAMILLA. Well, we're not fully fledged.

SUSAN. We're trainees.

DORIAN. I tried Buddhism last year. Decided orange just wasn't my colour.

CAMILLA. Drab's definitely not mine.

DORIAN. Great shades, though.

CAMILLA. Oh! Well, they're not strictly regulation.

SUSAN. Neither is begging, strictly. But we're on a mission to Chelsea and we've run out of money.

DORIAN. Chelsea?

CAMILLA. Just hoping the Lord will provide for transportation and refreshments.

She puts her hands in prayer and SUSAN rattles the tooth mug.

DORIAN. Well, I can provide both, if you don't mind sharing a cab?

CAMILLA. Really?

DORIAN. Truly.

SUSAN. Golly –

CAMILLA. Marvy!

CAMILLA/DORIAN/SUSAN.
> **Hello Chelsea!**
> **Goodbye Piccadilly!**
> **We're off for an exhilarating drive across the town**

CAMILLA.
> **Through the park and by the Thames**

DORIAN.
> **Past architectural diadems**

SUSAN.
> **And landmarks of renown**

CAMILLA.
> **Tell the Queen to wear her crown –**

COMPANY.
> **It's a cultural plunder-ful –**
> **Nights full of fun-derful –**
> **Lift up from under-ful –**
> **London**
> **It's a wonderful town!**

And away they go – with SUSAN *beginning to sense that three's a crowd…*

Scene Eleven

Chelsea flat.

DORIAN *ushers in exuberant* CAMILLA *and uneasy* SUSAN.

DORIAN. Make yourselves at home – all facilities at your disposal.

CAMILLA. How simply splendiferous!

SUSAN *glares at her, hands in prayer.*

SUSAN. Dost thou forget thy calling, Sister Camilla?

CAMILLA. What? Oh – whoops! Mea culpa, Sister Susan. I mean, Hallelujah! Praise the Lord!

SUSAN. Amen.

DORIAN *halts as he pops champagne.*

DORIAN. I say – are Jehovah's Witnesses allowed to drink?

CAMILLA. Oh yes, drink's fine. Holy spirit and all that. We're just not allowed to have lots of money or nice clothes.

SUSAN. Or boyfriends.

DORIAN. Talking of nice clothes – I really don't think I can stand another minute in this 'putting on The Ritz' kit. Give me five? Don't run off.

CAMILLA. Don't worry, we won't.

He dashes out – and CAMILLA *rounds on* SUSAN.

Look, we simply can't keep this up.

SUSAN. I agree. Let's just go.

CAMILLA. No, silly, let's just stay here and be ourselves.

SUSAN. What?

CAMILLA. He said all facilities at our disposal, which presumably includes a bathroom and guest bed.

SUSAN. You mean – stay here, with him?

CAMILLA. Why not? He seems perfectly civilised.

SUSAN. But now we're in Chelsea we can go in search of The Stairways Club.

CAMILLA. Oh, Susan, we don't even know if it really exists, never mind where.

SUSAN. Your mother said anyone could find it if they needed to.

CAMILLA. When my mother was an art student she was probably hallucinating on absinthe.

SUSAN. But we can't be ourselves with him.

CAMILLA. Well, not completely, obviously.

SUSAN. Then what's the point?

CAMILLA. Oh, stop being so difficult.

SUSAN. But why are you being so strange?

CAMILLA. Just don't pressurise me, Susan, or I shall get my tension earache.

She moves away, hands over ears.

SUSAN. Camilla – ?

DORIAN *returns, wearing trendy casual attire.*

DORIAN. Your host returns as himself.

CAMILLA *springs back to life, impressed.*

CAMILLA. Well, hello…

SUSAN *turns away to the bookcase, agitated.* DORIAN *pours champagne.*

DORIAN. Shall we drink to chance encounters?

CAMILLA. Yes, let's. Susan, what are you doing?

SUSAN. Reading poetry.

CAMILLA. We're drinking to chance encounters.

DORIAN. Cheers!

CAMILLA. Cheers!

DORIAN. Tell the truth, they're my sister's, actually. Books. Mad girl's an obsessive hotel-dweller, always up and off somewhere, no home life. So baby bro has to play host to her library. I mean, not that I don't read, but – well, photography's my big thing now.

CAMILLA. Really? It's mine too!

DORIAN. Studio's along the hall, I could show you around if you'd like –

SUSAN. Sorry, we're not allowed to look at photographs.

DORIAN. No?

CAMILLA. What?

SUSAN. Graven images and all that?

Awkward lull.

DORIAN. Your coats! So busy with the booze I forgot to unburden you. May I?

SUSAN. No thank you. We never take off our coats.

DORIAN. Never?

SUSAN. Not in public.

CAMILLA. Oh, drat this! I'm sorry, Dorian, but we've got a confession to make.

SUSAN (*warning*). Camilla –

DORIAN. Confession? Thought that was only the Holy Romans. So your lot do it too?

CAMILLA. We haven't a clue what they do, because that's our confession. We're not really Jehovah's Witnesses at all –

She slips off her coat to reveal basic school uniform, minus distinctive tie.

We're runaway schoolgirls!

DORIAN. Gosh!

CAMILLA. I'm sure if you knew the dire straits of our school you'd understand our desperate plight.

DORIAN. Actually, I'm all too simpatico. My sister's old school is under threat of extinction!

CAMILLA. You'd have to drive a stake through our Headmistress's heart to save ours. If only we'd finished our exams we'd never go back.

SUSAN. Camilla? What do you mean? We're never going back there, no matter what.

CAMILLA. Oh, be sensible, Susan. I can't have scarlet fever for ever.

SUSAN. But I don't give a fig about stupid exams any more.

CAMILLA. Yes you do. You give a very big fig because you want to go to university and so do I.

SUSAN. But I can't go *back*. That's why I had to run away!

CAMILLA. Oh, it'll all work out somehow. Don't let's think about it now. Just take your coat off and have a drink. Please?

SUSAN. I'm not taking my coat off until I can get changed out of my uniform.

CAMILLA. Get changed, then! Dorian, can Susan use your bathroom?

DORIAN. Of course! Last room on the left.

SUSAN exits with her case. CAMILLA *tries to cover.*

CAMILLA. Poor Susan, she's had a terrible time recently. A few days away will do her the world of good.

DORIAN. Good.

CAMILLA. Yes.

She catches his eye, both of them behaving slightly awkwardly.

DORIAN. More champagne?

CAMILLA. Why not?

He refills their glasses, then both speak at the same time.

CAMILLA/DORIAN. Dorian – / Camilla –

They laugh.

DORIAN. Ladies first.

CAMILLA. No, I was just going to say something silly.

DORIAN. So was I, actually.

CAMILLA. Well, I can't explain why, but I keep feeling there's something strangely déjà vu about you.

DORIAN. But that's exactly what I was going to say about you!

CAMILLA. Really?

DORIAN. Something about your voice…

CAMILLA. Nothing about your voice, some sort of *anima*…

DORIAN. Or the champagne – ?

CAMILLA likewise makes light.

CAMILLA. Yes, it's ridiculous!

They both turn away to look out of the window.

Gosh! This really is the most marvellous view.

DORIAN. Battersea Power Station.

CAMILLA. It looks like a great dark cathedral.

DORIAN. Or an upside-down elephant?

CAMILLA. Yes!

They catch each other's eyes again.

Can I ask you a probing personal question? Dorian.

DORIAN. If I may ask you one in return. Camilla.

CAMILLA. Well, Dorian –

DORIAN. Yes, Camilla?

CAMILLA. Oh, stop it, you'll give me the giggles.

DORIAN. Then I trust you'll give me them back.

CAMILLA *giggles*.

No please, do ask.

CAMILLA. But I can't now.

DORIAN. But I beseech you.

CAMILLA. But I want to ask you lots of questions.

Music 12. **I Know It's Asking a Lot**

DORIAN. So do I.

CAMILLA. But hundreds.

DORIAN. Me too.

CAMILLA. Go on then.

DORIAN. After you.

CAMILLA. No, after you.

DORIAN. But I don't know what to ask you first…

> **I know it's asking a lot**
> **To find out everything about you**
> **Even so, now you're on the spot**
> **I want to know what is your point of view**
> **I want to delve into your psyche**
> **I think I like imagining the way that we could be**
> **I know it's asking a lot**
> **But I have got to get to know you**

CAMILLA.

> **I know it's asking a lot**
> **To find out everything about you**
> **But oh, I'm wondering what**
> **Wondering, when, where, why, how and who?**
> **I want to know all of your history**
> **Don't be a mystery, satisfy my curiosity**
> **I know it's asking a lot**
> **But I have got to get to know you**

CAMILLA/DORIAN.

> **Now is the moment I've waited for**
> **How can I tell you that I adore you?**

They take off in a passionate tango.

> My life was incomplete
> You swept me off my feet
> Two perfect strangers meet –
> And ah-ah-ah-ah-ah-uh-oh…

They turn away from each other.

> I can't believe I said that

CAMILLA.
> Flirting about

DORIAN.
> Blurting it out

CAMILLA.
> Letting it all hang out

DORIAN.
> So much for Mr Cool

CAMILLA.
> I've been a total fool

DORIAN.
> How crass could I be?

CAMILLA.
> I'm not even free

CAMILLA/DORIAN.
> S/He'll think I do this all the time

DORIAN.
> Pick up a girl

CAMILLA.
> Hitch a ride

DORIAN.
> Give her a whirl

CAMILLA.
> Get inside

CAMILLA/DORIAN.
> **Rushing ahead when I ought to go slow**
> **Oh no, how low can s/he think I'll go?**

They face each other again, trying to act casually as if nothing's happened.

> **I know it's asking a lot**

CAMILLA.
> **To find out everything about you – bum-bum-bu-bum-bum**

DORIAN.
> **Bum-bum-bum-bum, to find out everything about you**

CAMILLA/DORIAN.
> **And so if you'd rather not**
> **I quite understand that's your point of view**

DORIAN.
> **It was only polite conversation**

CAMILLA.
> **With no implication**

CAMILLA/DORIAN.
> **Either of us meant it to be more**
> **I know it's asking a lot**
> **So I am not going to ask you**

DORIAN.
> **Bu-bu-bu-bum**

CAMILLA/DORIAN.
> **I'm not going to ask you**
> **No, I'm not going to ask you because I'm already sure.**

They fall into an embrace and their lips meet.

And SUSAN *re-enters, wearing sweater and slacks.*

SUSAN. I left my case in the… hall –

She reels as she takes in the scene.

CAMILLA. Susan…

SUSAN. What are you doing?

DORIAN. Fair question. I think we can only blame the arrows of Eros.

SUSAN. I'm not asking *you*. Camilla – ?

CAMILLA. Look, just don't – just –

SUSAN. Don't what? Don't *mind*?

DORIAN *struggles to catch up*.

DORIAN. Hey, no big deal. All my fault. Let's just – have another drink –

SUSAN. A drink?

DORIAN. Yes, come on. Have a drink and we'll all see the ridiculous side in a minute.

SUSAN. You don't know, do you? Tell him, Camilla. Tell him, you cheat.

CAMILLA. Oh, don't be such an utter baby.

SUSAN. Tell him!

DORIAN. Tell me what?

CAMILLA. Stop crowding me, Susan! I'm a free agent. So why don't you just grow up – and just – go and do your own thing.

SUSAN*'s devastated*.

SUSAN. I should have listened to Daimler, shouldn't I? Well, you'll never see me again, ever!

She bolts for the door and CAMILLA *pursues*.

CAMILLA. Susan, wait – oh, come back – I didn't mean it –

But SUSAN*'s gone*.

Blackout.

Scene Twelve

Chelsea Bridge.

Fog envelops the scene, as SUSAN *stumbles to a halt, delirious with despair.*

Music 13. **What Good is Life Without Love?**

SUSAN.
> **Everything's broken**
> **Everything's gone**
> **Everything's over**
> **From this moment on**
>
> **And if the sun never shone again**
> **I wouldn't care**
> **All I can see from now on**
> **Are the depths of despair...**
>
> **What good is life without love?**
> **There's nowhere left to run**
> **No way back to the way it was before**
> **The stars have fled from heaven above**
> **I thought she was the one**
> **No words of mine can reach her any more**
>
> **I would give anything to start this night again**
> **To wind the hands of Time**
> **Back to before that moment when –**

SUSAN *looks down into the abyss that beckons...*

> **What good am I without love?**
> **What reason left to breathe?**
> **One deadly kiss has cut my heart in two**
> **Accursèd Fate – I lay down my glove**
> **If I must take my leave**
> **With one step I'll prove my love was true**
>
> **I gave up everything I had to be with her**
> **Nothing I can do will take us**
> **Back the way we were**

The music swells as SUSAN *prepares to jump – then she pulls back as her nerve fails her, and crumples on the ground.*

> **I don't want to live**
> **I don't want to die**
> **Crying in the river till my tears run dry**
>
> **If there is a star**
> **To guide lost lovers by**
> **Show me where you are – please**
> **Won't you hear my cry...**

And her prayers are answered in a vision...

An expectant humming – turning into the throbbing of a mighty motorbike engine, coming closer, faster, louder.

A powerful headlamp sears through the fog like a search light. The engine stops.

SUSAN *watches in awe as* BUZZ BRAKELAST (*aka* MISS GIVINGS, *in glam-butch biker gear*) *swaggers into the light.*

BUZZ. Hi, kid. Buzz Brakelast, Emergency Breakdown Services, answering your call.

SUSAN. Sorry?

BUZZ. Lone female with blowout, no spare, requesting roadside rescue? Or are you saying it was a hoax?

SUSAN. I – I –

BUZZ. Well, make up your mind. Are you seriously stuck in need of assistance with your onward journey? Or just wallowing in self-pity before you phone home and tell your parents you're sorry?

SUSAN (*tearfully defiant*). I'll never ever say I'm sorry for being true to my heart. Even if I've lost everything, I still believe in love.

I just don't know where to find it...

BUZZ *lifts* SUSAN *up and away.*

Music 14. **The Stairways**

BUZZ.

> **Well you know things may not be as grim as they seem**
> **I could help you to dispel this bad dream**

> We could leave your troubles here to drift away
>   downstream
>
> When love has left you feeling hollow
> And life is all too much to swallow
> I'll take the lead if you'll follow me
> To a little place that I know
>
> When all you longed for is denied you
> Your heart is burning up inside you
> I'll be the angel to guide you home
> To a little place you should know…

Scene Thirteen

The Stairways Club.

The club and its glamorous gender-bending bohemian clientele materialise – as BUZZ *delivers* SUSAN.

CLUB-GOERS.
> The Stairways
> The Stairways
> The Stairways
> Everyone's waiting
> Everyone's waiting for you

SUSAN. The Stairways Club…?

She looks around in dazed wonderment.

It's just how I imagined it!

BUZZ.
> The moment that you walk through that door

CLUB-GOERS.
> The moment that you walk through that door

BUZZ.
> You're sure to find what you're looking for

CLUB-GOERS.
>What you're looking for tonight

BUZZ.
>So tonight

CLUB-GOERS.
>Come to the cabaret

BUZZ.
>Let your fancy take flight

CLUB-GOERS.
>We'll chase your cares away

BUZZ.
>Everything will be all right
>Leave your loneliness behind you
>And come where pain will never find you
>We're only here to remind you
>There'll always be a place you can go

CLUB-GOERS.
>The Stairways

BUZZ.
>A place where all your dreams can come true

CLUB-GOERS.
>The Stairways

BUZZ.
>And maybe some that you never knew…

CLUB-GOERS.
>The Stairways

BUZZ.
>Everybody's waiting for you

CLUB-GOERS.
>Everyone's waiting
>Everyone's waiting

ALL.
>Everyone's waiting for you

Dance break – SUSAN *with* BUZZ *and* CLUB-GOERS.

BUZZ.
> **If you need to drown your sorrow**
> **I've got a shoulder you can borrow**
> **Chill out and dance till tomorrow**
> **It's here inside The Stairways**

CLUB-GOERS.
> **All of your dreams can come true**

BUZZ.
> **Welcome to The Stairways**

CLUB-GOERS.
> **Everyone's waiting for you**

BUZZ.
> **Here inside The Stairways**

CLUB-GOERS.
> **Everyone's waiting**

BUZZ.
> **Come into The Stairways**

CLUB-GOERS.
> **Everyone's waiting, everyone's waiting**

BUZZ.
> **Welcome to The Stairways tonight!**

CLUB-GOERS.
> **The Stairways is waiting tonight!**

BUZZ. So here we are, my little stray.
> The fabulous Stairways Club and Cabaret.

> MARLENE (*aka* DORIAN, *in drag version of formal evening wear*) *comes to greet them.*

MARLENE. Buzz Brakelast!

BUZZ. Got another pick-up needs a pit stop.

MARLENE (*shrugs*). Ve never close.

BUZZ (*to* SUSAN). Kid, meet the legend who runs this joint.

SUSAN. Marlene Dietrich?

MARLENE. Enchantée.

SUSAN *shakes her hand, overawed*.

BUZZ (*to* MARLENE). Just learnt her first lesson in love, the hard way.

MARLENE (*to* SUSAN). Gave your heart to ze wrong girl, ja?

SUSAN *hangs her head*.

Zen ve must help you find ze right girl.

She clicks her fingers.

Camille – champagne for my guests!

CAMILLE (*aka* CAMILLA, *in French maid's uniform*) *sashays over with a tray of glasses*.

CAMILLE. Mais bien sûr, what else am I 'ere for?

MARLENE (*to* BUZZ). My new Mädchen. I zink I am – 'falling in love again'!

SUSAN *stares, as* CAMILLE *serves then raises a glass herself*.

CAMILLE. 'Ere's to – (*Turns to* MARLENE.) 'ow you say?

MARLENE. Chance encounters!

CAMILLE (*winks at* SUSAN). Salut!

BUZZ. Cheers!

SUSAN *is dumbfounded as they clink and drink to her*.

MARLENE. Enjoy ze show.

MARLENE *puts an arm round* CAMILLE *and steers her away – and* SUSAN *turns to* BUZZ, *confused*.

SUSAN. Why do I keep feeling everything means something more than it seems?

BUZZ. Work it out and wake up, kid.

SUSAN *is led away to a table, as –*

Music 15. **Fanfare and Sugar und Spice**

MARLENE *enters a spotlight.*

MARLENE. Good evening, ladies und ladies!

> **It's time to spring clean**
> **Put all zose dusty dreams avay**
> **I'm parading**
> **Masquerading**
> **Cos ze real life zing is so passé**
> **Ja –**
>
> **Zis little girl is made of sugar und spice**
> **Und all zings nice**
> **Cool as ice, so**
> **Don't let all zis goodness go to vaste**
> **Ven you could taste a little delight tonight**
> **Taste a little sugar und spice**

I look around and vot do I see…

> **Every night toujours la même**
> **Femme mit femme**
> **La crème de la crème**
> **But votever your heart's desire**
> **I vill set you on fire tonight**
> **Mit ein bisschen sugar und spice**
>
> **For La Dolce Vita Sackville-Vest**
> **I'm ze best in town**
> **And vunce you savour**
> **My heart's flavour**
> **You vill vant to Voolf me down**
>
> **Deine liebe Dietrich**
> **I turn ze free trick**
> **So how could you go wrong?**
> **For a little tête-à-tête**
> **Who needs Colette?**
> **Ven my French kisses go for a song**
>
> **Ja, zis little girl is made of sugar und spice**
> **Und all zings nice**
> **Cheap at ze price, ja**

> Don't let all zis goodness go to vaste
> Come on und taste a little delight tonight
> Taste a little sugar und spice
> Spice it up baby
> Taste a little sugar und spice
> Come on sugar
> Taste a little sugar...
> Sugar und spice.

Glamour is vot I sell.

The CLUB-GOERS *applaud.*

CLUB-GOERS. Encore, encore! More, more! Brava, brava!

MARLENE *takes a bow then silences them.*

MARLENE. And now... For ze seriously sad and lonely...

> A special act – for vun night only...
> Ze little bird viz ze cool blue tones –
> Ve proudly present –
> Miss Desiree Jones!

The CLUB-GOERS *applaud – as the music and lighting shift to moody blue – and* DESIREE *(aka* DAIMLER, *sleek and sophisticated in a cocktail dress) sits alone at the bar, drink in hand – and* SUSAN *is transfixed.*

Music 16. **What If?**

DESIREE.
> It's the end of the line, you're abandoned and blue
> A wallflower waiting to wilt
> Wondering why – was it them, was it you?
> Who should be feeling the guilt?
> Left as you are, bereft at the bar
> What's there to do but drink?
> But with every sip
> Comes a drip, drip, drip
> As you find yourself starting to think –
> What if...?

> What if the one that got away
> Was never really the one?
> What if this heartache is only a bruise?

A trio of CLUB-GOERS (*aka* JUDITH, LAVINIA *and* ANNABEL) *join her.*

TRIO.
Dooh-ooh

DESIREE.
What if despite the tears you shed

TRIO.
Doodly-ooh-dooh – wah

DESIREE.
You hear a voice inside your head

TRIO.
Doodly-ooh-dooh – ooh

DESIREE.
Saying maybe you only learn how to love when you lose…?

TRIO.
Doodly-ooh, doodly-ooh, doodly-ooh dooh
What if?

DESIREE.
What if that road you didn't take
Was only leading you on?

TRIO.
What if?

DESIREE.
What if this corner you're turning will turn out fine?

TRIO.
Dooh-ooh

DESIREE.
Not every road will lead to Rome

TRIO.
Doodly-ooh-dooh – wah

DESIREE.
Sometimes you need a way back home

TRIO.
> **Doodly-ooh-dooh – dooh**

DESIREE.
> **All that you have to do is follow the sign**

Dance break.

DESIREE/TRIO.
> **Oooh-ee-oo-ooh**

DESIREE.
> **What if?**

DESIREE/TRIO.
> **Oooh, ooh-ooh**

DESIREE.
> **What if the best is yet to come?**
> **Well wouldn't that be fun?**

TRIO.
> **What if?**

DESIREE.
> **What if tomorrow the skies will be blue – instead of**
> **you?**

TRIO.
> **Doo-ooh**

DESIREE.
> **What if that cloud was silver-lined?**

TRIO.
> **Doodly-ooh-dooh – wah**

DESIREE.
> **What if a girl can change her mind?**

TRIO.
> **Doodly-ooh-dooh**

DESIREE.
> **What if it's time to find somebody new?**

TRIO.
> **Somebody new**

The club and its clientele start to peel away.

DESIREE/TRIO.
What if?
What if?
What if –

DESIREE *aims her parting shot directly at* SUSAN.

DESIREE. I'm over you?

She exits after the others, leaving SUSAN *on her own as the vision fades.*

Scene Fourteen

Chelsea Bridge – Thursday night.

SUSAN *is in a new stew, as* CAMILLA *and* DORIAN *call out through the swirling fog.*

CAMILLA. Susan, Susan…

DORIAN. Susan, Susan…

SUSAN *spins as they rush in and find her.*

CAMILLA. Susan! Oh, thank goodness we've found you –

I thought something terrible – Oh, darling – I'm so sorry I've fallen in love with Dorian but please don't hate me.

SUSAN. I don't. I just need to get back to school and find Daimler.

CAMILLA. You mean you're in love with her now? But that's so neat!

SUSAN. It's a total mess! Because now she'll hate me for running away with *you* – but I can't go back to *her* without running into Bleacher.

CAMILLA. But that's what I'm bursting to tell you, Susan – the tyrant is about to be toppled!

SUSAN. What?

CAMILLA. Look at Dorian and think! Doesn't he remind you of someone?

SUSAN *gawps*.

SUSAN. Marlene Dietrich…

CAMILLA. Marlene Dietrich? Don't be silly. Dorian, give her a clue.

DORIAN (*in* BENNY'*s voice*). Uh – I'll come back laters. Sorry. Awright.

SUSAN. What?

CAMILLA. Benny the Bag! He was really Dorian in disguise on a secret mission! And Miss Givings was really his sister Diana!

SUSAN. What?

CAMILLA. Because Dame Dottie was their aunt and they're our new school governors!

SUSAN. What?

CAMILLA. I know, it's beyond incredible!

DORIAN. And made incomprehensibly complicated by labyrinthine legal precautions dear Aunt Dottie devised to protect her *own* headship!

SUSAN. What?

CAMILLA. But anyway basically, if we go back undercover tonight – and get the whole school to sign a petition tomorrow – then Bleacher's going to be banished under sub-clause – ?

DORIAN. Something –

CAMILLA. Something – and the only fly in the Germolene is Brenda Smears!

SUSAN *is completely flummoxed*.

SUSAN. What?

DORIAN. We'll explain in the car.

They exit.

Transition from night to next day:

Scene Fifteen

The school quad – Friday morning.

Music 16a. **Fly in the Germolene**

BRENDA *enters, gleeful.*

BRENDA.
> **This is going to be the best day of my life**
> **Ha-ha-ha-ha-ha-ha-ha...**

BRENDA *stands to attention as* MISS BLEACHER *enters.*

MISS BLEACHER. It's eight-thirty sharp. Where are all the boarders?

BRENDA. They must have had one of their midnight feasts, Miss.

MISS BLEACHER *fizzes.*

MISS BLEACHER. You see how the legacy of Bohemian decadence continues to corrupt this school, Brenda?

BRENDA. Yes, Miss.

MISS BLEACHER. Then don't just stand there, girl – go and rouse them!

BRENDA. Yes, Miss. Right away, Miss.

She scoots off.

Then MISS BLEACHER *is heralded by the merry whistling of 'Greensleeves' – as* MISS AUSTIN *enters on her bicycle.*

MISS AUSTIN. Good morning, Headmistress!

MISS BLEACHER *glowers*.

MISS BLEACHER. Thus far, Miss Austin, nothing about this morning seems good to me.

MISS AUSTIN. Really? When the golden sun salutes the morn? When birds do sing, hey ding-a-ding ding?

MISS BLEACHER. And the entire Upper Sixth bar Brenda Smears still lie asleep in their beds? Ding-a-ding.

MISS AUSTIN. Oh…

MISS BLEACHER. You and I need to have a serious discussion, Miss Austin. Kindly come to my study immediately you've completed roll-call.

MISS AUSTIN. But won't that delay you taking assembly?

MISS BLEACHER. I think you'll find I'm hastening the pace of change.

She exits. Then MISS AUSTIN *immediately perks up with spirited purpose and beckons in* SUSAN *and* CAMILLA.

MISS AUSTIN (*conspiratorial whisper*). So far, so relentlessly predictable, dear girls.

CAMILLA. And yet so totally utterly thrillingly scary!

MISS AUSTIN. Hence we must all keep our heads and stick to our battle plan. So – take the back stairs to the locker room and secrete yourselves there till I send for you.

CAMILLA/SUSAN. Yes, Miss.

They head off.

CAMILLA (*to* SUSAN). Isn't she simply splendid! I do hope when *I'm* that ancient I'll still inspire adulation.

Then DORIAN *and* DIANA *enter in* BENNY *and* MISS GIVINGS *guises, to hail* MISS AUSTIN *with urgent import.*

DORIAN. Seriously bad-news flash.

DIANA. Bleacher's drastically upped the ante.

MISS AUSTIN. Oh, good grief! What now?

DORIAN. I was just pretending to riddle a drain, when a
bulldozer pulled up on the playing fields –

DIANA. And a memo in my pigeonhole instructed me to assign
all games periods to callisthenics!

MISS AUSTIN. What? She's abolishing team sports for a
regimented Nazi-style health-and-fitness drill?

DIANA. So now we've not only got to save the school, we've
got to save the First Eleven!

DORIAN. And before the navvies start laying the tarmac!

MISS AUSTIN. Well, I'm only a few signatures short of a
petition. But the speedy conversion of Brenda Smears calls
for a spur of Damascene proportions… Any ideas?

DIANA and DORIAN exchange blank looks.

DIANA. Just crack on and hope we come up with a corker.

MISS AUSTIN. Right-o.

She sprints off and DORIAN turns to DIANA.

DORIAN. Is Damascene about swords, or is that Damoclean?

DIANA. Just think blindingly spectacular.

DORIAN. Right. Um…

They rack their brains.

DIANA. What would dear Aunt Dottie do now, if she were
me…?

Then suddenly – PING! They both know the answer.

Music 16b. **What Would Dottie Do?**

Get your kitbag and ladder. Then meet me in Matron's office.

They sprint off separately.

Scene Sixteen

Locker room.

CAMILLA *enters, declaiming, followed by a distracted* SUSAN.

CAMILLA.
>We few, we happy few, we band of sisters;
>For she to-day that sheds her blood with me
>Shall be my sister – be she even so vile as Brenda
>   Smears –

SUSAN. I can't even think about saving the school if I lose Daimler.

CAMILLA. Of course you can't, Susan.

SUSAN. I've got to go and find her.

CAMILLA. No, you've got to stay put. That's why I sent Daimler a note via an underling to sum up the situ so she can find you.

SUSAN. What?

CAMILLA. And lo – here she comes!

>CAMILLA *conceals herself, as* DAIMLER *enters, reading a note.*

SUSAN. Daimler – ?

>DAIMLER *looks up and they lock eyes – then both speak at the same time.*

DAIMLER/SUSAN. Please don't think –

>*Awkward beat.* SUSAN *tries to make light.*

SUSAN. Snap!

DAIMLER. So there we are! What more proof could I need that 'our hearts now beat as one'?

>*She screws up the note.*

Well, sorry to spoil the plot. But just because you've lost Camilla that doesn't mean you automatically get me.

CAMILLA *peeks out, confounded.*

SUSAN. Oh, Daimler, I'm so sorry. I've been so stupid.

DAIMLER. You have. You've also been blind, insensitive, selfish and rather shallow.

SUSAN. I know. But I didn't mean to be. Oh, I just need to talk to you.

DAIMLER. Then that's too bad. Because I'm sick of being your trusty confidante.

SUSAN. But you're everything to me now. Oh, Daimler, you always knew you were the right girl for me, didn't you?

DAIMLER. Well, the boat's sailed, Susan, and I wasn't on it. So let's just go back to being friends. All that matters now is saving the school.

DAIMLER *turns her back* – SUSAN *reels in dismay – and* CAMILLA *erupts from her hiding place.*

CAMILLA. Oh no – please don't turn this into a tragedy.

Both SUSAN *and* DAIMLER *turn on her.*

DAIMLER/SUSAN. Camilla!

CAMILLA. Then it's all my fault, isn't it? I'm the cloven-hoofed beast who tore you apart…

I'm practically as evil as Bleacher, aren't I?

Oh, I just totally and utterly hate myself…

She slumps on the bench and wails.

SUSAN. This is *my* crisis, not yours, Camilla…

DAIMLER *grabs a towel and thrusts it at* CAMILLA.

DAIMLER. Here – use this.

CAMILLA. No, it's all right, I've got a handkerchief.

DAIMLER. I mean to take a cold shower and do some character-building.

CAMILLA *balks – looks to* SUSAN *– but* SUSAN *sides with* DAIMLER. CAMILLA *sighs.*

CAMILLA. Well, I do feel rather grubby…

She slings the towel over her shoulder, and exits to the showers with dignity.

SUSAN *turns to* DAIMLER.

SUSAN. Daimler – couldn't we just start again?

DAIMLER. I wish we could. But I know I'll never be the right girl for you, Susan, even if I should be.

SUSAN. Why?

DAIMLER. Because if we're going to be horribly honest about it, I just don't do the magic for you, do I?

SUSAN *is stunned – and spurred*.

SUSAN. Oh, darling – you couldn't be more wrong!

Music 17. **You Do Do the Magic For Me**

You do do the magic for me
Isn't it tragic I couldn't see
I was blinkered then
But now I think again
And you do the magic for me

DAIMLER *resists,* SUSAN *pursues.*

You do hasten my heart with your smile

DAIMLER.
Funny how you never told me that before

SUSAN.
Although you've been here all this while

DAIMLER.
For you to ignore!

SUSAN.
I didn't recognise
That look in your eyes
And now I'm standing on trial

DAIMLER.
And I'll be judge and jury

SUSAN.
>It may be hard to believe but
>For the first time
>I'm sure of what I'm feeling
>No, there's no concealing
>
>You – have the power to see right through
>Everything that I say or do
>So I know you must know it's true

SUSAN gives DAIMLER her best puppy-dog look.

>Don't you?

DAIMLER sighs.

DAIMLER.
>I do...

DAIMLER/SUSAN.
>Phew!

They link hands and dance à deux.

DAIMLER.
>You do make me go weak at the knees

SUSAN.
>Look out, I'm gonna knock you off your feet

DAIMLER.
>Although I know there are no guarantees

SUSAN.
>And no retreat

DAIMLER.
>I just can't resist

SUSAN.
>Don't even try –

DAIMLER.
>This is what I've missed

SUSAN.
>So have I!

DAIMLER.
>**Cos you do do the magic –**

DAIMLER/SUSAN.
>**You do do that magic**
>**You do do the magic for me.**

>*Romantic kiss.*

>CAMILLA *re-enters, draped in towel, bedraggled but*
>*reinvigorated.*

CAMILLA. Bravissima! Now all we've got to do is switch the
snitch and slay the dragon.

>*Music 17a.* **Switch the Snitch**

>*They brace themselves and exit.*

Scene Seventeen

Sixth-form dorm corridor.

ANNABEL, LAVINIA *and* JUDITH *are holding* BRENDA
*hostage inside a laundry basket, much against her will and
theirs.*

BRENDA *squeals from within the basket, as* LAVINIA *sits
atop it.*

BRENDA (*off*). Let me out!

JUDITH. We want to let you out, Brenda.

ANNABEL. Like yesterday, man!

LAVINIA. We just need you to cooperate and let us.

>*Howls from* BRENDA.

JUDITH. Oh, come on, Brenda, don't you want to be a Nobel
Prize-winning astrophysicist in your own right, not just the
wife or mother of one?

BRENDA. I want to get out of this basket!

ANNABEL *gives up.*

ANNABEL. Sorry, cats. I'm a peacenik. I can't do this. Let the bird fly.

LAVINIA *and* JUDITH *exchange looks, as* BRENDA *howls.*

LAVINIA. Your call.

JUDITH. Abort.

LAVINIA *gets off the basket – and a furious* BRENDA *pops up and clambers out.*

BRENDA. You beasts! Well, guess who won't be a prefect when Miss Bleacher makes *me* Head Girl.

MISS AUSTIN *enters.*

MISS AUSTIN. Oh, Brenda, have you still not got the message?

JUDITH. She just won't listen, Miss.

MISS AUSTIN. Well, I suspected it might require amplification.

She beckons in SUSAN, CAMILLA *and* DAIMLER, *bearing placards and a large roll of paper.* BRENDA *gapes to see* SUSAN *and* CAMILLA.

BRENDA. What are they doing back here?

MISS AUSTIN. What we're all doing except you, Brenda – our Dosserdalian duty!

BRENDA *recoils as the* GIRLS *hoist placards – saying* 'AGE QUOD AGIS!' 'SAVE OUR SCHOOL!' 'UP THE ART ROOM!' 'DEATH TO HOMECRAFT!' 'PUPIL POWER RULES!' 'DAME DOTTIE'S FOREVER!' – and MISS AUSTIN *takes up a tambourine.*

Music 18. **Do Your Bit**

> **There's a whole revolution that is on its way**
> **Starting here and it starts today**
> **Now every girl has their part to play**
> **So come on – do your bit**

UPPER SIXTH.
>Do your bit

MISS AUSTIN.
>Like the women of the ATS

UPPER SIXTH.
>Do your bit

MISS AUSTIN.
>When the call came we said yes

UPPER SIXTH.
>Do your bit

MISS AUSTIN.
>Like Amy flying high

UPPER SIXTH.
>Do your bit – better do it now

MISS AUSTIN.
>You've got to reach up to the sky

JUDITH.
>There's a brand-new feeling that is in the air

LAVINIA.
>And it won't be long before it's everywhere

ANNABEL.
>So come on Brenda, now don't be square

JUDITH/LAVINIA/ANNABEL/MISS AUSTIN.
>Girl, you've got to do your bit

UPPER SIXTH.
>Do your bit

MISS AUSTIN.
>Like Christabel and Emmeline

UPPER SIXTH.
>Do your bit

MISS AUSTIN.
>You've got to get out on the scene

UPPER SIXTH.
Do your bit

MISS AUSTIN.
When the finger points at you

UPPER SIXTH.
Do your bit – better do it now

MISS AUSTIN.
You know what you've got to do

The UPPER SIXTH *unfurl the petition – saying 'We Think Miss Bleacher is a Horrible Headteacher' and covered in columns of signatures and inkblots – and* MISS AUSTIN *proffers a pen.*

UPPER SIXTH (*continues under dialogue*).
Do it, do it – come on now
Do it, do it – come on now
Do it, do it – come on now
Do it, do it, do it, do it

MISS AUSTIN. So, Brenda – united we stand or fractured we fall. There's only one way we can save the day. All for one and one for all.

BRENDA *looks at the petition and the pen, sceptical.*

BRENDA. You mean I could really make all the difference? Me?

GHOSTLY VOICE. Yes, Brenda, you!

There's a collective gasp as all look up – to see the spectral figure of DAME DOROTHEA.

DAME DOROTHEA. You ARE the missing link.

We are each of us born into history
Upon the shoulders of those who came before
Fearless women who fought for all that's sisterly
Now we must raise up their baton once more

Will you – Brenda Smears
Seize this chance?
To be respected by your peers
Remembered down the years

> **Hark – do I hear three cheers**
> **As you join our proud advance?**

UPPER SIXTH. Hip hurrah! Hip hurrah! Hip hurrah!

DAME DOROTHEA.
> **So that all our future daughters may go far…**

The GIRLS *hum solemnly, underscoring* BRENDA*'s potential conversion to the cause.*

BRENDA. This could be the turning point for my entire life and the underpinning of my future self-esteem and ability to form meaningful relationships without resentment and insecurity with a full understanding of the sociopolitical-cultural context of my upbringing. Couldn't it?

DAME DOROTHEA (*impatiently*). Yes, Brenda. Yes, this is that moment.

All await BRENDA*'s decision… But she declines the pen –*

BRENDA. Give me that tambourine!

And grabs it from MISS AUSTIN.

> **I'm ready –**
> **I'm ready –**
> **Ready to rock this world**

BRENDA *unleashes her inner rebel.*

> **There's a whole revolution that is on its way**
> **And it's starting here and it starts today**
> **Now every girl has their part to play**
> **And I'm going to do my bit**

All go with the new flow.

DAME DOROTHEA/UPPER SIXTH.
> **Do your bit**

MISS AUSTIN/BRENDA.
> **Like Christabel and Emmeline**

DAME DOROTHEA/UPPER SIXTH.
> **Do your bit**

DAME DOROTHEA/UPPER SIXTH.
You've got to get out on the scene

DAME DOROTHEA/UPPER SIXTH.
Do your bit

MISS AUSTIN/BRENDA.
When the finger points at you

DAME DOROTHEA/UPPER SIXTH.
Do your bit – better do it now

MISS AUSTIN/BRENDA.
You know what you've got to do

ALL.
Do it, do it
Do, do it, do it

BRENDA.
I want to do it now

DAME DOROTHEA. Then do!

All try to point headbanging BRENDA*'s attention to pen and petition.*

MISS AUSTIN/UPPER SIXTH.
Do it, do it
Do, do it, do it

BRENDA.
I want to do it now

MISS AUSTIN/UPPER SIXTH.
Do it, do it
Do, do it, do it
Do-do-do-do-do-do-do-do-do...

BRENDA.
Do it, do it, do it, do it, do it –

MISS AUSTIN *pulls her up.*

MISS AUSTIN. Please just sign the petition, Brenda.

BRENDA. Oh – right – yes, Miss –

BRENDA *takes the pen and signs – to great relief all round.*

MISS AUSTIN. To victory!

ALL.
> **Do your bit!**

DAME DOROTHEA*'s ghost disappears and* MISS AUSTIN *heads the* GIRLS *out – then she turns back to exchange thumbs-up with* DIANA, *in makeshift Suffragette costume, and* DORIAN, *her sound and lighting assistant.*

Then MISS AUSTIN *dashes off after the* GIRLS *and the* DOSSERDALES *dash off separately.*

Music 18a. **Do Your Bit – play-off**

Scene Eighteen

The Headmistress's study.

MISS BLEACHER *is at her desk.*

Knock at the door. She hides the photo frame.

MISS BLEACHER. Come!

> MISS AUSTIN *looks in.*

MISS AUSTIN. Um – would you rather see me first or Susan Smart, Headmistress?

MISS BLEACHER. What?

MISS AUSTIN. Oh – did I fail to mention she's come back to sit her Oxbridge entrance?

MISS BLEACHER. Susan Smart is back in this school?

MISS AUSTIN. I felt sure she wouldn't dash our high hopes for her future.

MISS BLEACHER. *I'll* determine her future, Miss Austin. And it's time to put you out to pasture.

MISS AUSTIN *'reels'*.

MISS AUSTIN. You don't mean – hang up my gown? But, Headmistress –

MISS BLEACHER. Oh, skip the sob stuff. Just bring her in and bow out.

MISS AUSTIN *withdraws and* SUSAN *enters*.

Well, Susan Smart – assuming parental pressure has prompted your return, I trust you're ready to make a swift confession.

SUSAN. Then you're wrong about everything, Miss Bleacher. Because I refuse to be judged by you and all I regret is running away.

MISS BLEACHER *grimaces*.

MISS BLEACHER. Then how right I was to regard you as a corrupting influence. And I shall expel you this instant unless you give me the name of the other girl.

SUSAN. Then it's my duty not to give a damn what you do to me, Miss Bleacher, because I'd rather die for this school than help you destroy it.

Before MISS BLEACHER *can respond, there's a knock at the door and* MISS AUSTIN *looks in*.

MISS AUSTIN. Sorry to pop back in, Headmistress, but Brenda Smears says she's learned something vitally important pertaining to the matter in hand.

MISS BLEACHER. I'm dealing with the matter in hand, Miss Austin. And I need nothing further from Brenda Smears.

BRENDA *barges in*.

BRENDA. But I was wrong to tell you what I did about Susan, Miss.

MISS BLEACHER. What do you mean, girl?

BRENDA. I mean I take it all back, Miss. Because it's my duty as a member of this school not to betray another member, Miss.

MISS BLEACHER *bristles*.

MISS BLEACHER. You're clearly ill, Brenda. Report to
    Matron at once.

BRENDA. But I've never felt better about myself, Miss. Look
    at me!

    MISS BLEACHER *recoils as* BRENDA *performs a*
    cartwheel – then there's another knock at the door.

MISS AUSTIN. Me again.

MISS BLEACHER. What now?

MISS AUSTIN. Camilla Faraday, Headmistress. She wants to
    confess to being the other girl.

MISS BLEACHER. What?

    CAMILLA *makes a dramatic entrance.*

CAMILLA. Oui, c'était moi, Miss Bleacher. And it is a far, far
    better thing I do now than I have ever done. For no greater
    love hath any girl than to lay down her life for her friend. I
    am in your hands – not only guilty but gloriously
    unrepentant. Do with me what you will!

    MISS BLEACHER *glints.*

MISS BLEACHER. Be sure I shall. (*To* BRENDA.) And since
    I've bagged both culprits by their own admission, Brenda,
    you can consider yourself entirely expendable.

    BRENDA *stands her ground – and there's another knock at*
    the door.

MISS AUSTIN. So sorry, Headmistress, but Daimler Jones says
    she wants to confess to being the other girl.

MISS BLEACHER. What?

    DAIMLER *enters, cool as a cucumber.*

DAIMLER. Because I *am* the other girl now, Miss Bleacher. So
    if you expel Susan and Camilla, you'll have to expel me.

    JUDITH, LAVINIA *and* ANNABEL *enter.*

JUDITH. And hereby so say we all, Miss Bleacher.

LAVINIA. Each and every girl in this school.

ANNABEL. Cos when the chips are down we are all the other girl!

They present the petition – and MISS BLEACHER *takes stock of it and them.*

MISS BLEACHER. Well! You *have* been busy little bees, haven't you? But I still fail to see what you hope to achieve.

She tosses the petition aside.

Whole-school detention. Assembly hall. Now!

MISS AUSTIN *sighs.*

MISS AUSTIN. A short course in dramatic structure would so assist your interpretive skills. But if I have to spell it out – this is when we turn the tables, so now it's chips for you.

UPPER SIXTH. Boo!

MISS AUSTIN. And all that's left to do is tie up the loose ends.

Enter DIANA *and* DORIAN, *as themselves.*

DIANA. Which is where we come in, Miss Bleacher.

MISS BLEACHER. And you are who?

DIANA. I am Diana Dosserdale and this is my brother Dorian.

MISS BLEACHER. Just a minute –

DORIAN. Yes, you know us better as Benny the Bag –

DIANA. And Miss Givings, the temporary games mistress.

MISS BLEACHER. Then what – ?

DIANA. As I'm sure you're aware, Miss Bleacher, our uncle's recent death has left the governorship of the school in a state of hiatus, since my brother and I can only inherit when we're both of legal age.

DORIAN. Which you've no doubt calculated gives you a clear run for another two years till my twenty-first birthday.

MISS BLEACHER. So I repeat, then what – ?

DIANA. Then our lawyers informed us that Sub-clause Twenty-three of the School Constitution allows me to act as sole governor pro tem in 'Exceptional Circumstances' –

DORIAN. Viz. your flouting virtually every precept this school stands for –

DIANA. With the unanimous disapproval of your pupils –

DORIAN. Proof of which we went undercover to obtain –

DIANA. As now conclusively verified by our lawyers in this telegram. Which – with the constitutionally required quorum of prefects present – gives me the right to demand your immediate resignation, Miss Bleacher.

She hands telegram to MISS BLEACHER, *who studies it.*

MISS BLEACHER. I see… How very unfortunate… that I must crush your hopes once again.

She rips up the telegram.

MISS AUSTIN *sighs.*

MISS AUSTIN. Really, you can't just keep on throwing your toys out of the pram, you know.

MISS BLEACHER (*fierce*). I never *had* a pram!

(*Composes herself.*) But I do have this…

She produces a parchment scroll.

A codicil to Sir Digby Dosserdale's will, signed and witnessed on his deathbed, as per Sub-clause Twenty-four – guaranteeing me, Beatrix Bleacher, lifetime tenure in this Headship, no matter what.

EVERYONE ELSE. Gasp!

MISS BLEACHER *hands the scroll to* DIANA.

MISS BLEACHER. Please do run it past your lawyers. I'm sure they'll agree it trumps your telegram.

DIANA *and* DORIAN *unravel the scroll and stare at it in shock, watched by* MISS AUSTIN *and the* GIRLS.

MISS BLEACHER *gloats.*

What was it you said I needed to learn about dramatic denouement, Miss Austin?

DORIAN. Uncle Digby must've lost even more marbles than we knew.

DIANA. He must have been drugged to put his name to this.

MISS BLEACHER. His fatal flaw, like yours, was to believe your liberties would last for ever.

JUDITH (*to* DIANA). Is she right, Miss?

The DOSSERDALES *exchange looks and shrug defeat – and* MISS BLEACHER *glints.*

MISS BLEACHER. Me right, you wrong, everybody out except these two.

She points to SUSAN *and* CAMILLA *– and exodus is about to commence but* BRENDA *raises her hand.*

BRENDA (*to* DIANA). Can I just ask a question, Miss?

DIANA. We've all got questions, Brenda. Such as how could any educated woman so conspire to subjugate her own sex?

MISS AUSTIN. How could our solicitors have contrived to leave our flank so exposed?

DORIAN. How come we didn't even know there *was* such a loopy loophole?

MISS BLEACHER. Loopy or not, legal and binding it is. Hard cheese. Chip-chop.

BRENDA. But I wanted to ask if it's still binding if you're not legally Miss Bleacher, Miss.

MISS BLEACHER *stiffens.*

MISS AUSTIN. What do you mean, Brenda?

BRENDA. Because what if she's not, Miss?

MISS BLEACHER (*fierce*). Listen to me, not that deluded misfit. I said out! Now!

DIANA. Wait!

MISS AUSTIN. Please get to your point swiftly, Brenda.

BRENDA. I mean she's really Miss Enid Baden-Bulcock, Miss.

MISS AUSTIN. What?

DIANA. Not *the* Enid Baden-Bulcock – ?

DORIAN. Who?

DIANA. The adopted foundling and experimental subject of the infamous child psychologist, Dr Enoch Baden-Bulcock?

> MISS BLEACHER *freezes*.

DORIAN. Not *that* Dr Enoch Baden-Bulcock? Dear Aunt Dottie's fanatically anti-Suffragist arch-enemy?

MISS AUSTIN. How do you know this, Brenda?

BRENDA. I had a rummage in her drawers, Miss.

MISS AUSTIN. What?

BRENDA. I know it's bad form, Miss, but – look!

> BRENDA *whips open the desk drawer and holds up the photo frame – to reveal the sepia image of a fearsome old madman in his study.*

> That's him, isn't it? And it says on the back in her handwriting: 'Dearest Daddy, thy will *will* be done.'

EVERYONE ELSE. Gasp!

> *All turn to stare at* MISS BLEACHER.

MISS AUSTIN. You poor soul – that's why you said you never had a pram…

DIANA. You were raised in a cage, weren't you?

DORIAN. And now you oblige us to send you to jail…

BRENDA. But you could learn before you depart, Miss, if you promise to change your ways?

MISS BLEACHER. Change?

DAIMLER. It's never too late to change yourself.

MISS BLEACHER. Never?

SUSAN. Not if you really want to.

MISS BLEACHER. Really?

MISS AUSTIN. Well I don't doubt you'd need some help, but –

DORIAN. Even you could 'do well in what you do', couldn't you?

DIANA. If you went back to teaching chemistry?

CAMILLA. And just stop being horrid and say you're sorry.

All await her response in hopeful expectation.

But MISS BLEACHER *holds her head high in steely disdain.*

MISS BLEACHER. Me? Ask forgiveness from you?

Music 19. **I Ask for Nothing**

> **I ask for nothing**
> **And I am satisfied**
> **I've no illusions**
> **No dreams to be denied**
> **I don't care if you like me or not**
> **There is nothing I want that you've got**
>
> **I wait for no one**
> **To run and comfort me**
> **I am sufficient**
> **In my own company**
> **There are no empty hopes in my hand**
> **This is it now I know where I stand**
>
> **Faith is for fools and for losers**
> **Waiting their turn in the line**
> **See them fall for the cheats and the users**
> **Casting pearls before swine**
> **I will take what is mine**
>
> **I ask for nothing**
> **I don't owe anyone**
> **My score is settled**
> **And I know what I've done**
> **There is no room for doubt in my mind**
> **No forgetting what I left behind**

Time never heals what is broken
Just drags you on down the road
And for all the good words that are spoken
None will lighten your load
Or pay back what you're owed

I ask for nothing
So don't you pity me
My eyes are open
And I know what I see
I don't care if you like me or not
There is nothing I want that you've got

So come on, take me
You'll never break me
Go on, do it, just try
Damn me, hate me
But don't underrate me
You won't ever see me cry
Not I
Nothing
Never
No one
Not ever

Your weakness will always be my strength.

Goodbye.

She exits.

MISS AUSTIN. That poor sick woman…

DIANA. She's beyond our help…

DORIAN. But at least she's gone…

Pause – then MISS AUSTIN *raises a 'V' for victory.*

MISS AUSTIN. We may allow ourselves a brief period of rejoicing.

ALL. Hurrah!

DIANA. And we can now give these girls their rightful leader. Miss Austin, I would like to offer you the Headship of this school. Will you accept?

MISS AUSTIN. I should be honoured and delighted – on one
condition. That you instruct Messrs. Put-their-foot-in-it and
Partners, Solicitors, to sling their quills and putt off.

DORIAN. My pleasure!

DIANA. And we can blow the whistle on those bulldozers.

MISS AUSTIN. Then let us spur ourselves upwards and
onwards with a hearty rendition of the School Song – (*To
pianist.*) Con gusto, Miss MacLaren!

Music 20. **The School Song / Best Days reprise**

ALL.

> **A school for life we shall always know**
> **However life unfurls**
> **Whate'er our strife and where'er we go**
> **We're Dosserdalian girls**
>
> **Never ceasing to pursue**
> **The good and true in all we do**
> **United one and all**
> **We rally to our sisters' call**
>
> **And come what may**
> **We'll save the day**
> **The Dosserdalian way!**
>
> **Bring back the best days**
> **Sparkle-and-zest days**
> **Riding-the-crest days**
> **We will see those days again**
> **Freely expressed days**
> **Just be-my-guest days**
> **Oblige-noblessed days**
> **On with our quest**
> **Roll on the best days of our lives!**

The End.

Music 21. **Bows / Navy Knicks – curtain**

Music 22. **Playout**